TWISTERN

50 Twisted Western Movies

FIRST EDITION

Visit our website, www.Twistern.com

ISBN-13: 978-0-615-62472-3

Designed by Ronin Productions, Inc.

Table of Contents

PREFACE

What do zombies, aliens, and robots have to do with gunslingers, tumbleweeds and showdowns? Like peanut butter and chocolate, the mixture of science fiction, horror, comedy, musical, and psychedelic genres with the classic Western results in a delicious concoction. This produces something that couldn't exist without combining these seemingly disparate and contradictory elements. I call this mixed genre *Twisterns* or twisted western movies. It may not be part of your regular movie watching regime, but if you're a rabid movie fan like me, you're probably aware of it.

What exactly is a twisted Western movie?

Well, a Western movie is one that takes place in or references (in one way or another) the American Old West in the latter half of the 19th century. The twisted part comes into play when another genre (or subgenre) is injected into the mix. Instead of the tried and true McCoys versus the Hatfields, Indians versus cowboys, and other familiar plot formats, there might be zombies, samurai, vampires, ghosts, or other fantastical creatures interwoven into the script. Or, it might be set in an unfamiliar geographical location, such as in outer space, the Australian Outback, or in modern times. Importantly, *Twisterns* adhere to the Western ethos and there is always some clear reference to the Western movie formula. Sometimes it's a distant connection, but it's there.

There are surely movies that would seem like a glaring error of omission on my part from this book. The classic sci-fi Western *Star Wars* is a good example. For example, the Han Solo character is clearly based on, characterized as, and dressed as a gunslinger. And the classic Spaghetti Westerns of Italy also seemingly qualify as twisted western movies. But they follow the standard Western drama pattern or are so well known and beloved that they have been omitted.

It is interesting to note that there are not many, if any, writers, producers, actors, or directors that made more than one foray into the *Twistern* subgenre. The market for such films is smaller and the films tend to be less profitable in the mass marketplace, a trend I hope is broken like a wild horse in the future. There is many a wayward tumbleweed left to still unturn.

I hope that after you read each brief description you will choose to seek these films out in whatever form is convenient to you and decide your likes or dislikes on your own. *Twistern* fans are definitely an opinionated bunch of cowpokes and cowgirls.

So, strap on your rocket cowboy boots, holster your six-gun loaded with silver bullets, and enjoy *Twistern: 50 Twisted Western Movies*!

Kelly Knight
May, 2011

BACK TO THE FUTURE PART III

(1990)

Directed by Robert Zemeckis
Written by Robert Zemeckis and Bob Gale

Actors:
MICHAEL J. FOX
CHRISTOPHER LLOYD
THOMAS F. WILSON
MARY STEENBURGEN
LEA THOMPSON
ELISABETH SHUE
MATT CLARK
HARRY CAREY JR.
JAMES TOLKAN
FLEA

Building on the enormously profitable and popular *Back to the Future* franchise, Marty McFly (Michael J. Fox) and Doctor Emmett "Doc" Brown (Christopher Lloyd) travel back to 1885 to avert the certain death of Dr. Brown at the hand of drooling madman, Buford "Mad Dog" Tannen (Thomas F. Wilson).

When Marty arrives, the DeLorean time machine's fuel line is damaged, forcing him and Doc Brown to come up with a plan to push it up to the required 88 miles per hour with a train. Unfortunately, the track that they have to follow ends in a bridge over a valley that has yet to be built. If they miscalculate, Marty and the DeLorean will be dashed to bits on the rocks far below.

While they prepare the car for the task, they try to find the perpetrator of Doc Brown's death. At the town festival, Doc Brown reconnects with Clara Clayton (Mary Steenburgen), whom he'd previously rescued from a runaway wagon. When local bad guy “Mad Dog” Tannen tries to horn in on the obvious affection between them, things get rough and Marty intervenes before Mad Dog kills Doc.

After the encounter with Mad Dog, they discover that they have once again altered history. A photograph of Doc’s grave featuring his name on the headstone changes to read Marty’s name. Our heroes now must deal with the disturbing fact that they’ve tainted time and save Marty instead of Doc.

Now part of a new destiny, will Mad Dog kill Marty in a duel and take Clara from Doc? Will Doc and Marty be able to repair the time-traveling DeLorean and return to the future?

The sixth highest grossing movie when it was released in 1990, *Back to the Future Part III* went on to make over $300 million internationally and in rentals. This is not surprising, especially with Executive Producer Steven Spielberg’s name attached to the project. Made for approximately $40 million, the production values are high. Though the special effects look dated by modern standards, primarily due to the chromakey compositing, this is still a movie that is clearly made at a big name studio. The sets are complex, have lots of depth and detail and are fun to look at.

Inspired by Michael J. Fox’s desire to explore the Old West with the Marty McFly character, director Robert Zemeckis and co-writer Bob Gale created a plausible script with plenty of references to the Western genre and cues from the previous two *Back to the Future* movies. Other than some occasional foul language, this is a fun one for the whole family.

Mad Dog: “What's your name, dude?”

Marty McFly: "Uh, Mar- Eastwood. Clint Eastwood."

Mad Dog: "What kind of stupid name is that?"

BILLY THE KID VS. DRACULA

(1966)

Directed by William Beaudine
Screenplay by Carl K. Hittleman

Actors:
JOHN CARRADINE
CHUCK COURTNEY
MELINDA PLOWMAN
VIRGINIA CHRISTINE
MARJORIE BENNETT
WILLIAM FORREST
HARRY CAREY JR.
WALTER JANOWITZ
BING RUSSELL
OLIVE CAREY
ROY BARCROFT
HANNIE LANDMAN

Lisa Oster (Hannie Landman) and her immigrant parents Eva and Franz (Virginia Christine and Walter Janowitz) are traveling in the West, seeking a better life. One night, as the campfire slowly fades, a vampire (John Carradine) bites her on the neck. Her highly superstitious, old world parents are distraught.

Later that evening, a stagecoach picks up a mysterious, gaunt and extremely well dressed stranger. The other passengers consist of a whisky salesman, the widow Mary Ann Bentley (Marjorie Bennett) and her brother, James Underhill (William Forrest). When Mrs. Bentley shows the stranger a picture of her daughter Betty, he takes a sinister interest in everything about the lovely young woman.

Unbeknownst to the stagecoach folk, they've inadvertently picked up the evil blood sucker. When they layover at a way station to water the horses and catch some shut eye, the vampire disappears. A friendly Indian tribe camps nearby, but is not a threat to the white folk.

The next morning, a squaw is found dead, her jugular punctured, and the tribe is enraged. They assume that the people in the stagecoach caused the death and they hunt down and massacre them all. Taking advantage of the tragedy that he purposefully caused, the vampire steals James Underhill's identity documents.

At the Double Bar B Ranch, Betty Bentley (Melinda Plowman) runs things with the assistance of the foreman, William "Billy" Bonney (Chuck Courtney). She is fully aware of who Bonney is, the famous outlaw Billy the Kid. But, Billy has changed his ways and the two plan to marry.

A wrench in the works is Dan "Red" Thorpe (Bing Russell), Betty's former boyfriend. Not only has Dan lost his girl, but he also lost his job since he was the foreman until Billy showed up. Now he's just itching to make his rival feel his pain, which he attempts at every opportunity.

Betty is distraught when she learns of the stagecoach massacre that included her beloved mother. But, she is comforted when her Uncle James shows up, whom she has never met before. This is not her uncle, of course, but the vampire masquerading as him.

The Oster family finally arrives at the ranch and they immediately raise the alarm that something is amiss.

Will the vampire kill or convert Betty into one of the undead? Will Billy listen to the Osters' warnings, figure it out in time and stop him? What if Dan prevents Billy from protecting Betty?

Often shown as a double feature with *Jesse James Meets Frankenstein's Daughter*, this low budget film was one of director William "One Shot" Beaudine's final works. Beaudine was famous for refusing to shoot more than one take, whether it needed it or not. Mistakes, inconsistencies, and downright flubs were no reason to go off schedule, to unintentionally hilarious results. *Billy the Kid vs. Dracula* was shot in a paltry 8 days and it shows. The writer who came up with the ludicrous story, Jack Lewis, sold the script to Carl K. Hittleman for the princely sum of $250, who then took credit for it. This was a wise move on Lewis's part, though neither man wrote much thereafter.

This is a B-movie, *Twistern* classic, complete with rubber bats, wooden acting, grade Z cinematography, and special effects squeezed out of a ketchup packet. But, Carradine's portrayal of the unnamed vampire is eerie, and his skeletal face and satanic visage is imminently watchable. Also on display is Courtney's horse riding skills, which are fantastic.

Don't miss the absolutely comical showdown where Billy and the vampire face off in the finale. It sure takes a lot to put a determined blood-sucking parasite down…or does it?

Prop up your dusty boots after a long day on the range, make yourself a bloody Mary and don't forget that this movie sucks in all sorts of cheesy, hilarious ways. Fangs for reading!

BLAZING SADDLES

(1974)

Directed by Mel Brooks

Screenplay by Mel Brooks, Norman Steinberg, Andrew Bergman, Richard Pryor, and Alan Uguer

Actors:
CLEAVON LITTLE
GENE WILDER
SLIM PICKENS
HARVEY KORMAN
MADELINE KAHN
MEL BROOKS
COUNT BASIE
DOM DELUISE

When John Wayne, the King of all movie cowboys, politely declines to be in your Western comedy, it can be a bit disappointing. But when he says he would be first in line to see it, you know you've struck gold. Wayne knew this would be an all-time classic but thought it was too risqué for his image.

This film swings at racial stereotypes with the subtlety of a sledgehammer. But, what did you expect from the man who brought us *The Producers, History of the World Part 1* and *Young Frankenstein*? Mel Brooks, the genius that he is, took the Western genre and turned it on its ear with one of the best comedies ever, Western or otherwise.

Hedley Lamarr (Harvey Korman) is a conniving, scheming State Attorney General who wants to buy all of the land along the new railroad route. He knows that they will have to come to him for the land and pay his demanded exorbitant prices.

Rock Ridge is one of his targeted towns and a new sheriff is hired to protect against this brigand. He happens to be a black man who was about to be hanged. But, he's hired because the hope is that it will incite the townspeople to lynch him (as sheriff) or just pack up and vacate, leaving the town easy pickings for Lamarr.

Instead, Sheriff Bart (Cleavon Little) and his sidekick Jim, "The Waco Kid" (Gene Wilder) befriend the townspeople and they give them 24 hours to come up with a plan to get them out from under the thumb of Lamarr.

What he comes up with could only be dreamed up by the likes of Mel Brooks and Richard Pryor with a whole lot of snorting, guffawing, and "Hey, you know what would be *really* funny…!?!"

They decide to build a replica of the town, fill it with dynamite and blow the bad guys to kingdom come. But, their scheme doesn't pan out without a little difficulty…

The film breaks movie-making conventions; the "fourth wall" is broken during a brawl that spills out into the Warner Brothers studio lot and it has to be seen to be believed.

Several other titles for the film were rejected, such as *Tex X* (as in Black Muslim leader Malcolm X), *Purple Sage, Black Bart* and there are infamous stories of wild script parties that involved drugs and excessively loud music. The studio was concerned about Richard Pryor's increasingly erratic behavior, which resulted in his replacement by Little as the Sheriff.

There are constant references to classic Western films in *Blazing Saddles,* spoofing many of the greats. See if you can spot the homage to *High Noon, Destry Rides Again,* and *Once Upon a Time in the West.* The film was shot on the same set as another *Twistern* classic, *Westworld.*

In 2006, the Library of Congress selected *Blazing Saddles* for preservation due to its being "culturally, historically, and/or aesthetically significant."

Jim, The Waco Kid, says, "I must have killed more men than Cecil B. DeMille. It got pretty gritty. I started to hear the word 'draw' in my sleep. Then one day, I was just walking down the street when I heard a voice behind me say, 'Reach for it, mister!' I spun around... and there I was, face-to-face with a six-year old kid. Well, I just threw my guns down and walked away. Little bastard shot me in the ass. So I limped to the nearest saloon, crawled inside a whiskey bottle, and I've been there ever since."

Saddle up your rubber chicken and ride!

COWBOYS & ALIENS

(2011)

Directed by Jon Favreau

Screenplay by Roberto Orci, Alex Kurtzman, Damon Lindelof, Steve Oedekerk, Mark Fergus, and Hawk Ostby

Actors:

OLIVIA WILDE
HARRISON FORD
DANIEL CRAIG
ADAM BEACH
SAM ROCKWELL
KEITH CARRADINE
CLANCY BROWN
PAUL DANO
WALTON GOGGINS
DAVID O'HARA
ANA DE LA REGUERA
NOAH RINGER

A cowboy (Daniel Craig) wakes up in the middle of the desert with complete amnesia, a gut wound, and a strange device strapped to his wrist. When three ruffians stumble upon him and try to rough him up, he responds violently, killing them. He rides one of the horses into a nearby tumbleweed town where he's patched up by Preacher Meacham (Clancy Brown), meets a mysterious woman named Ella Swenson in a bar (Olivia Wilde), and runs afoul of Colonel Woodrow Dolarhyde, a wealthy and ruthless rancher (Harrison Ford) and his crazy son Percy (Paul Dano).

Somebody woke up on the wrong side of the ranch!

Things progress quickly from there; turns out that the cowboy is a wanted criminal named Jack Lonergan, who is accused of stealing gold from the Colonel. Before everything can go right down the toilet, alien spaceships suddenly attack the town, bombing the main street and capturing people with long, whip-like mechanical tentacles. With the sudden appearance of the spacecraft, Lonergan's odd device around his wrist starts to glow and he discovers that he can shoot at the aliens with it. Normal guns don't work, but this does.

After the dust clears, a posse is formed to chase after the kidnapped folk. Against his wish to beat the daylights out of Lonergan, the Colonel decides that the power of the weapon on his wrist outweighs any other desire at the moment.

Based on the graphic novel of the same name by Scott Mitchell Rosenberg and directed by noted director Jon Favreau, this was a production with a huge budget, somewhere in the neighborhood of $163 million dollars. And it shows with the incredible special effects, tight editing and cinematography, stellar cast, and marvelous soundtrack by the talented Harry Gregson-Williams. Steven Spielberg was one of the executive producers.

So, does it all work? You bet! This is a non-stop rollick through Rosenberg's creation, brought to life on the silver screen. And it's a doozy of a *Twistern*. There's a wonderful theme of two sworn enemies brought together to conquer an unknown antagonist, mixed with pure Western genre elements, fast paced action scenarios, evil aliens trying to take over the world and even some moments of horror straight out of movies like *Predator* and *Aliens*.

There are even racial and interpersonal relationships explored, adding depth to what is essentially an action film.

The only disappointment was the lesser roles given to Clancy Brown, Adam Beach, and Sam Rockwell, actors that can carry a movie all by themselves. Brown's character, Preacher Meacham, is never fleshed out. Beach plays Nat Colorado, Colonel Dolarhyde's right hand man. There's a great father-son subplot between the two characters that's fun to watch these two superb actors play out. Rockwell plays Doc, a saloon owner. Unfortunately, this role seems to have been written with someone else in mind and it comes across as miscast. Of course, Rockwell is an amazing actor and makes the best of what he's given, resulting in a performance that isn't distracting at its worst.

There are some fun references to *Raiders of the Lost Ark*, a tip of the hat to Harrison Ford and Steven Spielberg's iconic Indiana Jones action film franchise.

The exterior shots were filmed at Plaza Blanca, the New Mexico location where several other notable Westerns were filmed. The scenes are breathtaking, pure Old West. *Cowboys & Aliens* is quite possibly one of the best *Twisterns* ever made and it's an absolute must see!

Jake declares, "We were flying."

"Yeah," agrees Ella.

Jake intones, "I don't want to do that again."

"No," Ella replies emphatically.

COWBOYS & ZOMBIES

(2011)

Directed by Rene Perez
Written by Rene Perez

Actors:
DAVID A. LOCKHART
CAMILLE MONTGOMERY
RICHARD MORA
ROBERT AMSTLER

The year is 1849, during the gold rush, and Mortimer (David A. Lockhart) is a bounty hunter on a mission. He purchases a young woman named Rhiannon (Camille Montgomery) to use as bait to capture an Indian named Brother Wolf (Richard Mora) who is accused of raping and murdering a girl. He tracks the Indian to a field and ties Rhiannon to a stake in the middle of it.

Meanwhile, two prospectors discover a glowing meteorite buried in a hillside. They dig it up and take it into the community of Jamestown; everybody that lives and works there gathers around. One of the prospectors breaks it open with a pick, and green gas and particles explode outward, infecting anyone within spitting distance, turning them into flesh-eating zombies.

Back at the field, Brother Wolf and Mortimer duke it out, and the bounty hunter prevails, shackling Brother Wolf and taking the three of them back to Jamestown. When another bounty hunter named The German (Robert Amstler) tries to steal Brother Wolf away from Mortimer, he handcuffs the wanted Indian warrior to a tree. The two bounty hunters run off to exchange hot lead. While they're fighting, Brother Wolf is attacked by a zombie. Rhiannon saves him and they escape together, only to be recaptured by Mortimer when The German is also attacked by a zombie.

Brother Wolf and Mortimer decide to call a truce for the sake of survival. When the trio arrives in town, they find it deserted with all of the windows boarded up. Will they live to tell the tale or will they be overrun by zombies before next sunrise?

Originally released direct to video as *The Dead and the Damned* and attempting to capitalize on the big budget release of *Cowboys & Aliens* and the zombie fad sparked in the early 2000s, this low-budget independent picture has nothing to do with that film other than the *Twistern* theme. Made for a paltry $30,000 (in comparison to $163 million), *Cowboys & Zombies* is a good example of how the current state of technology allows for higher quality production value in movies made on a shoestring budget.

Lockhart's character always seems surprised that he's got a gun in his hand, which seems odd for a bounty hunter. He's constantly surprised when he runs out of bullets and can't ever seem to deal with a jammed weapon. Maybe this is on purpose, to give the character more depth, but it does seem a bit too greenhorn. Both Lockhart and Mora have distinctly out of place accents that are not period appropriate, which will be distracting to some viewers. But it is possible to look past it and enjoy the creative, well-paced script and action.

For a *Twistern,* there is a surprising amount of nudity in *Cowboys & Zombies*. The surprising thing is not that it is present here, but that it isn't more prevalent in the *Twistern* genre in general, given the exploitative nature of the subgenre.

A scene towards the end of the film where our hero is plugging oncoming zombies is filmed from his perspective, giving it a video game feel. The cinematography here is perhaps purposefully referencing a *Twistern* first person shooter game like the *Red Dead Redemption* series, for example. Usually, we see video games mimicking movies, but here we have the reverse and to great effect.

Director-writer Rene Perez and cinematographer Paul Nordin chose to film in truly stunning Northern California settings, much to the benefit of the movie. Perez and producer Mattia Borrani also composed a country-rock and atmospheric soundtrack worthy of a much larger budget picture.

So, here's another extremely low budget *Twistern* for all you dudes and dudettes. If you're in the spirit, you could do a lot worse. Slide on your armored chaps, strap on two bandoliers, and aim for those zombie heads!

"Cowboys, Indians and zombies made the Wild West even wilder!"

CURSE OF THE UNDEAD

(1959)

Directed by Edward Dein

Screenplay by Edward Dein and Mildred Dein

Actors:
ERIC FLEMING
MICHAEL PATE
KATHLEEN CROWLEY
JOHN HOYT
BRUCE GORDON
JIMMY MURPHY

Writer/director Edward Dein and his wife Mildred originally came up with this concept as a movie titled *Eat Me Gently* as a joke. The concept was a humorous Old West satire about a homosexual vampire cowboy running around the desert eating little boys. Universal Pictures picked it up and after only 18 days of filming, a surprisingly serious treatment of the original theme emerged.

Preacher Dan Young (Eric Fleming) sits by the bedside of a sick girl. It looks like she'll live the night. But, when he leaves the room momentarily, she dies. When the Preacher examines her neck, he sees two small circular wounds. Was this the cause of her death or did she die from natural causes?

They're not too bright in this town, cowpokes.

Meanwhile, Doctor John Carter (John Hoyt) keeps losing young female patients to some sort of mysterious sickness. When the doctor arrives home after a long night, his irate son Tim (Jimmy Murphy) tells him how their nearest neighbor, Buffer (Bruce

Gordon), has been sabotaging their land by damming a stream. When Tim tried to unblock the water, Buffer and his gang beat him up and shot his hat. (You should never shoot a man in the hat. It irritates him to no end.)

After he calms Tim down, Doc Carter rides into town to talk to Sheriff Bill (Edward Binns) about what can be done about the rapscallion, land-grabbing Buffer. Unbeknownst to him, he's being shadowed by a mysterious cowboy named Drake Robey (Michael Pate). Doc leaves and the sheriff unsuccessfully talks to Buffer about his behavior. When Doc's dead, lifeless body arrives home in the seat of his horse-drawn buggy with his throat torn open; Tim and his sister Dolores (Kathleen Crowley) are beside themselves with grief.

After they bury their father and leave the mortuary, the spooky cowboy in black reappears and climbs into the crypt with the dead body.

Also known as *Mark of the West,* the plot of *Curse of the Undead* is a murky mess. Drake Robey ends up working as a ranch hand for Dolores Carter – but only at night because of his "condition." The sheriff is killed mysteriously, but nobody seems all that concerned (clearly, he was not well liked).

Preacher Dan senses that evil is afoot, but can't pin down who or what is causing all of the havoc. He has the hots for Dolores, but admits to her that he would be crazy not to wed her for her money. Will Preacher Dan and Dolores consummate their romance or will the menacing doom overtake them?

Meanwhile, Tim is killed by Buffer. But once again, his sister doesn't seem to care.

Everything comes to a head when Dolores hires Robey to kill Buffer. Will Robey snuff out Buffer? Is he a vampire or not? What are his motives? Does he just want to drink blood or is he a cowboy hit man?

The acting is pretty bad. The editing is abrupt, cutting off scenes randomly. The directing is 50s television quality. The music consists of somebody who discovered a Theremin lying around. What does this all add up to? Why, a classic *Twistern* of course!

Don't forget your silver bullets and cross!

DEAD BIRDS

(2004)

Directed by Alex Turner
Written by Simon Barrett

Actors:
HENRY THOMAS
ISAIAH WASHINGTON
MARK BOONE JUNIOR
PATRICK FUGIT
NICKI AYCOCK
MICHAEL SHANNON

When a Civil War detail tries to make a deposit at a bank in Fairhope, Alabama, their transaction is interrupted by William (Henry Thomas) and his gang of outlaw Confederate soldiers, who brutally murder everyone and make off with the gold. But their escape does not go smoothly and they kill an innocent little boy on their way out of town.

When they arrive at a remote farm house to hole up for the night, they are attacked by a strange beast. They kill it, but the evil that permeates the place has them by its grasp. When they discover gold inside, things just go from bad to worse.

What is in the haunted house and what's the deal with the gold? Will the gang be able to resist the evil within or will the evil within them be the thing to destroy and consume?

Using sets built for Tim Burton's fantasy adventure drama *Big Fish* and set in 1863, *Dead Birds* was shot in three weeks with a $1.5 million budget. The film has a similar feel to *The Burrowers*. The supernatural elements emulate the works of famed horror author H.P. Lovecraft.

The sparse, echoing soundtrack created by Peter Lopez also adds to the foreboding tension. The subtle, spooky sounds build tension in the classic manner of the horror movie genre.

This was the first feature film for director Alex Porter. He does an excellent job with the superb cast and writer Simon Barrett's leisurely paced, yet highly intriguing script. Cinematographer Steve Yedlin shot a polished, gloomy film filled with a dark atmosphere of dread and creepiness. The special effects are particularly good-looking, computer generated or otherwise. This is clearly where many of the budgetary pesos were allocated.

Twistern fans will recognize much of the cast, including Patrick Fugit, Michael Shannon, Mark Boone Junior, Nicki Aycox, and Isaiah Washington. A lesser cast would not have been able to pull this movie off as well. Mark "Boonie" Boone Junior and Michael "Showboat" Shannon had such a great time on the set of *Dead Birds* that a six-minute short was made about them and included on the DVD as a hidden extra.

This is a good one to watch in the middle of the day, unless you're brave enough to watch it in the middle of the night. Just remember, "There are worse things than dying."

Katy, bar the door!

DEAD MAN

(1995)

Directed by Jim Jarmusch
Screenplay by Jim Jarmusch

Actors:
JOHNNY DEPP
GARY FARMER
CRISPIN GLOVER
LANCE HENRIKSEN
MICHAEL WINCOTT
JOHN HURT
ROBERT MITCHUM
IGGY POP
EUGENE BYRD

William Blake (Johnny Depp) arrives in the company town of Machine for his new job as an accountant. But, the head boss (Robert Mitchum in his final role) has already filled the position and dismisses him violently. Blake is distraught and falls in with a former prostitute. When they are discovered by her jealous ex-boyfriend, there's a shootout. Blake is injured, flees on a stolen horse and three killers are hired to track him down.

And that's just the beginning of this psychedelic *Twistern*! There's more plot in this movie than most, but it proceeds at a leisurely pace. There's a slow unfolding of the story that involves tragedy, murder, cannibalism, poetry, beauty, racism, sadness, and confusion. References to the poet William Blake, whom our character is mistaken for, are woven throughout the movie.

This is also one of the few movies that attempt to represent Native Americans in a realistic light, going so far as to *not* subtitle or dub their languages. Instead, viewers are left to guess what is being said, just as they would in real life.

The cast is a who's who of really interesting actors, even in the supporting roles. And they do a spectacular job, especially Gary Farmer as the Native American named Nobody.

This was director/writer Jim Jarmusch's sixth film and just as different and unique as his other work. Here, he works extremely hard to bring something new to the table and he's thoroughly successful. Jarmusch has been quoted as saying that he's most interested in "the non-dramatic moments in life." *Dead Man* does a fine job of sliding towards the next event, with none of the emotional peaks and valleys of the typical Hollywood film. Shot in sepia tone, the visual experience is like falling into an old time photo. You know the kind. Where none of the subjects smile and they all look like they'd rather be somewhere else.

The soundtrack is famed musician Neil Young meandering along on a guitar, primarily. There's no sense of beginning, middle, and end in the music and that suits this movie experience just fine. Blake doesn't always know where he is in the continuum of his own life and the music reflects his uneasy existence.

If you enjoy being rewarded as a film viewer for recognizing symbolism and metaphors, you're going to love this film. If you just want to go along for one of the weirdest (but not just for the sake of being weird) movies you've ever seen, skip the peyote and fire this one up!

"That weapon will replace your tongue. You will learn to speak through it. And your poetry will now be written with blood," said Nobody (to William Blake).

DUDES

(1987)

Directed by Penelope Spheeris
Screenplay by Randall Jahnson

Actors:
JON CRYER
DANIEL ROEBUCK
FLEA
LEE VING
CATHERINE MARY STEWART

Three punk rockers grow tired of New York City and decide to head out West to channel their inner cowboy and Indian. Jon Cryer plays self-destructive Grant, who is supported by his two friends. Biscuit (Daniel Roebuck) is a big, teddy-bear kind of guy who just wants to have a good time and eat dog biscuits. Milo (Flea) sees Grant being sucked into a deep hole of depression and puts up the money to make the journey to Los Angeles, where he hopes there's a better life for all three of them.

Before the trio makes it to the City of Angels, they run across a crew of rednecks who brutally murder Milo. Led by the evil Missoula (Lee Ving), the killers roar off into the desert after chasing Grant and Biscuit far from any salvation. Grant sees a vision of a cowboy on horseback, who leads them out of the arid wasteland. They eventually find help from the lovely, single, and tough as nails Jessie (Catherine Mary Stewart).

Jessie patches the boys up, outfits Grant as a gunfighter, Biscuit as a Mohawk'ed Indian warrior and they give chase to Missoula and his gang. Before they find them, they lay over at an abandoned ghost town and consume some "Snake Oil". Hallucinating, they see visions of an Indian village being slaughtered by Civil War soldiers led by Missoula himself.

Will they track down Missoula and avenge Milo's death? Will Jessie and Grant fall in love? What do Grant's visions of the mysterious cowboy mean?

This modern *Twistern* mixes punk rock culture with a Western thriller to a soundtrack split between cowpunk and heavy metal originals and cover songs. However, noted director Penelope Spheeris doesn't seem to be able to make *Dudes* work quite as well as her other movies, such as *Suburbia* and *Wayne's World.* Here, the production is uneven, the dialogue sometimes a bit stilted, and there is a general air of 80s pastiche.

Still, Cryer and cast really throw themselves into the mix and it's undeniably fun to watch them work. It's nice to see Cryer playing Grant with a real edge, a change from most of his roles as a sweet, naive innocent. This is a kid that could easily end up dead, either by his own hand or someone else's. It would be nice to see what he could do with a bad guy role or a role with more depth.

Only Stewart's character seems unreal and cartoonish. The explanation of why and how she ended up in that location, doing what she's doing and surviving around men who are barely one step above crazed animals is too obviously a plot device to enable Grant and Biscuit to accomplish the predictable and inevitable shoot out. Also, the psychedelic moments in the film are entertaining, and while they give a unique twist to the film, they also come across as cartoonish, wandering into the realm of unintentional comedy.

And yet, there are moments of real brilliance worthy of the *Twistern* genre and this would make a great double feature with *Near Dark*. If you like 80s metal and punk, make sure you get a copy of the soundtrack featuring Megadeth and The Vandals.

EL TOPO

(1970)

Directed by Alejandro Jodorowsky
Screenplay by Alejandro Jodorowsky

Actors:
ALEJANDRO JODOROWSKY
BRONTIS JODOROWSKY
JOSE LEGARRETA
ALFONSO ARAU
MARA LORENZIO

Be warned. This is the most depraved and disturbing *Twistern* ever. The imagery is so bizarre and intentionally unsettling, that most viewers will want to hightail it out of there long before the final credits. And yet, there is a metaphysical beauty to it all, connecting deeply to the inner workings of mankind and its need to destroy as well as love.

Proceed ahead if you have the constitution for it.

A mysterious rider dressed in black named El Topo (Alejandro Jodorowsky) rides the desert with a tiny, naked, 7-year-old boy (Brontis Jodorowsky) in the saddle with him. When they stop and dismount, El Topo declares to the boy, "Now you are 7. Now you are a man," and insists that he bury his teddy bear and a picture of his mother in the sand. Afterward, they mount back up and set off again.

Soon, they come to a village where every man, woman, child, and animal has been brutally slaughtered. They find one last dying inhabitant who begs them to kill him. El Topo hands his gun to the tiny child and has him finish the man.

After they leave the village, El Topo and the boy are attacked by three perverted outlaws who like to lick and shoot ladies' shoes, slice up bananas with a Calvary sword, and other bizarre activities. El Topo ends up gunning them down, but not before he learns that they are part of the gang responsible for all the death in the village, a group lead by "The Colonel" (David Silva).

He tracks down and confronts The Colonel and the remainder of his gang, who have holed up at a monastery where they physically and mentally torture the monks and kill the inhabitants at random. El Topo frees the monks and castrates The Colonel, who commits suicide. When he decides to ride off with The Colonel's woman, Mara (Mara Lorenzio), he leaves the little boy behind, much to the boy's sorrow and consternation. Thankfully, the boy will be looked after by the peaceful monks.

Mara convinces El Topo to seek out and challenge four gun masters and they wander around the desert until they come across the first, a blind man who is aided by a legless man strapped to an armless man. The blind man is unaffected by bullets, but the aftermath of the duel ends with El Topo striding away from their shallow graves.

The second master is a gypsy who lives with his mother, keeps a full grown male lion as a pet, forges copper plates and creates intricate, delicate geometric structures. El Topo is defeated by the gypsy, who does not kill him. But, El Topo eventually figures out a way to trick him and kills him and his mother.

His encounters with the third master, a musician surrounded by rabbits, and the fourth master, a weaponless aboriginal gunfighter, are equally eccentric.

And that's just the first half of the movie! *El Topo* is, at its best, a great metaphysical journey seeking enlightenment similar to the writings of Carlos Castaneda. At its worst, there is so much freaky weirdness to make it nearly incomprehensible.

Populated by deformed and maimed actors, perverse sexual situations, and riddled with religious and philosophical references, *El Topo* is an underground film for underground film fanatics. It will never be mistaken for a widely released film. Yet, it has great beauty and will make the spiritually hearty *Twistern* fan sit up and notice. Like the works of Frederico Fellini, Salvador Dali, and other "off kilter" artists, it's full of mind-altering, breath-taking images. It may also cause nightmares and dry heaving.

El Topo was released on DVD in 2007, almost 40 years after it premiered. Alejandro Jodorowsky wrote, directed, starred, and composed the music (with Nacho Mendez) and there have been rumors that a sequel is in the works.

This is one *Twistern* you won't soon forget, so make sure your ten gallon hat is on tight. This is one bucking bronco and you're in for a wild ride.

"Who are you to judge me?" questions The Colonel.

"I am God!" declares El Topo.

FROM DUSK TILL DAWN 3: THE HANGMAN'S DAUGHTER

(1999)

Directed by P.J. Pesce

Screenplay by Alvaro Rodriguez and Robert Rodriguez

Actors:

DANNY TREJO
ORLANDO JONES
MICHAEL PARKS
TEMUERA MORRISON
MARCO LEONARDI
REBECCA GAYHEART
ARA CELI
SONIA BRAGO
JORDANO SPIRO
LENNIE LOFTON

"When Gabriel blows his trumpet, I shall be playing the tuba." - Ambrose Bierce

When sardonic American journalist Ambrose Bierce (Michael Parks) stops in a small Mexican village for a drink, he witnesses the hanging of Johnny Madrid (Marco Leonardi). Johnny is accused of bedding down the beautiful Esmeralda (Ara Celi), the daughter of the sadistic local executioner called The Hangman (Temuera Morrison).

At the last moment a stranger shoots the rope, freeing the swinging Johnny. They ride off with Esmeralda, her psychotic father in hot pursuit.

None of this is of particular interest to the seemingly insensitive Ambrose, who leaves soon after in pursuit of the legendary

Pancho Villa. In the stagecoach, he meets a straight-laced couple who are traveling the West spreading Christianity (Rebecca Gayheart and Lenni Lofton).

Soon, the newly freed Johnny is back to his old outlaw ways. When he and his gang of cutthroats rob the stagecoach, the missionary couple and Ambrose escape into the desert. Scorching in the rays of the burning sun, they stumble upon an abandoned brothel that rises like a mirage out of the sand. It turns out that it isn't uninhabited, though, and soon the place is filled with scoundrels and whores. Running the joint is a barman named Razor Charlie (Danny Trejo) and a strangely seductive madam named Quixla (Sonia Braga).

Meanwhile, looking for some more debauchery, Johnny and his gang show up and odd things start happening. Not long thereafter, The Hangman and his posse also appear on the scene.

But as soon as the ruckus begins, it's revealed that the inhabitants of the brothel are all merciless vampires.

Will the two warring groups kill each other or will they band together to avoid being devoured by the vampires? What special secret regarding Esmeralda contains the answers to what's going on?

Filmed with a budget of $5 million, *From Dusk Till Dawn 3: The Hangman's Daughter* is a prequel to the original and was released direct to video. Quentin Tarantino and Robert Rodriguez (who co-wrote the story with his cousin, Alvaro Rodriquez) were producers once again. Their touch is distinctly felt in the pacing and vivid violence.

Like the first two installments, many of the same elements are present here. Despite the brutality and sadism, there are moments of levity supplied by characters like Ezra Traylor (Orlando Jones), a hairbrush salesman. The absurdity of a salesman of seemingly unwanted merchandise wandering around a barren desert is never really explored. Frankly, it doesn't matter as Jones adds a monumental lisp to his character purely for comedic value. Yeehaw!

Don't miss sticking around for the credits, where the raison d'etre of the film is revealed. Watch for it!

So, break out your garlic and crosses and stake a claim on the couch for this bloody vampire *Twistern* you can really sink your teeth into!

GHOST TOWN

(1988)

Directed by Richard Governor
Written by Duke Sandefur and David Schmoeller

Actors:
FRANK LUZ
CATHERINE HICKLAND
JIMMIE F. SKAGGS
PENELOPE WINDUST
BRUCE GLOVER
LAURA SCHAEFER
ZITTO KAZANN

A young woman (Catherine Hickland) drives wildly down a desert road alone, throwing a wedding veil out of the open top of her convertible Mercedes. When she pulls over because of a blown tire, a dust cloud envelopes her and something in the swirling dirt grabs her and drags her away. A jewel eyed crow watches from a nearby branch, a herald of evil.

Meanwhile, Deputy Langley (Frank Luz) has the music cranked up to ten on his Walkman and is out shooting old cars, bottles, and cans for target practice. He misses the Sheriff's call for action on the CB radio at first, but then hears it and speeds to the scene where they discover the young woman's car with its paint sand blasted off and half buried. Where is she and is she still alive?

Langley follows horse tracks out into the desert and soon stumbles on an old headstone. When he moves it, a skeleton comes up out of its' shallow grave croaking, "You're the one. You'll rid my town of the evil!"

He escapes the bony ghoul and rambles into an old, deserted ghost town, where he spends the night. In the morning, he wanders around and discovers human remains everywhere he looks. Stumbling from one building, he sees a cowboy standing in the middle of the street. He yells a greeting to the man, but he disappears in broad daylight, only to reappear sitting in a rocking chair on a nearby porch.

Langley starts to talk to him and discovers that he is The Dealer (Bruce Glover), who spews forth a bunch of cryptic nonsense, then disappears again.

Soon, Langley discovers that the entire town is populated by ghosts, caught between heaven and hell because of the resident evil gunslinger Devlin (Jimmie F. Skaggs). Devlin is the one responsible for the missing young woman, who he sees as a former scorned lover and plans to do bad things to her.

Ghost Town is another low-budget production, this time from the late 80s, which still allows for the sets, cinematography, and script to be pretty complex and sophisticated. Only the acting is B-grade, which isn't too surprising given the lack of big-name actors. Still, they do this horror *Twistern* a service and treat the entire shindig seriously.

Directed by Richard Governer, this is his one and only film credit and most likely a pseudonym for a director that didn't want anything to do with it at some point. That explains the rather rambling twists and turns in the script, the unoriginal soundtrack, and the somewhat herky-jerky flow of the editing.

This was also one of noted producer Charles Band's films made under the Empire International Pictures label, which also pumped out *Ghoulies, The Puppetmaster, Trancers,* and other great B-movies.

It's rumored that *Ghost Town* was inspired by the movie *Curse of the Undead,* though it has few to no actual similarities. In *Curse of the Undead,* you have vampires. In *Ghost Town,* you get ghosts. The antagonist in both movies is supernatural and that's about it.

As of this writing, *Ghost Town* is not available on DVD and well worth your time to seek this one out.

GRIM PRAIRIE TALES

(1990)

Directed by Wayne Coe
Written by Wayne Coe

Actors:
BRAD DOURIF
JAMES EARL JONES
WILLIAM ATHERTON
MARC MACLURE
SCOTT PAULIN
TIM SIMCOX
WILL HARE
MICHELLE JOYNER
LISA EICHHORN
WENDY J COOKE
JENNIFRE BARLOW

"Hit the trail…to terror!"

Farley (Brad Dourif) is a clerk riding his horse out West to meet up with his wife in Jacksonville, where she tends to his sick mother. One evening, a rough-and-tumble bounty hunter named Morrison (James Earl Jones) rides up to his campfire, an unexplained dead man Morrison calls Charlie strapped to his pack mule. They proceed to spend the night trying to outdo each other with grim prairie tales.

Morrison's first story involves Lee (Will Hare), a grizzled old cowpoke who attempts to cut across a Native American cemetery to save some time. Unsurprisingly, it turns out to be a big mistake.

After Farley hears the first story, he hungers for more and coerces another from Morrison.

The second story tells the tale of Tom (Marc Maclure), a traveler that kindly takes a young pregnant woman under his wing. She's clearly lost and afraid, so he offers her shelter and food. Little does he know that she's more than she appears.

Farley can hardly contain himself after the second story and decides that he'd like to tell one of his own. This one revolves around a pioneer family (featuring William Atherton) that lays claim to a prime piece of land out West. Everything seems fine and dandy until the horrific legacy that they left behind rears its ugly head once again.

Well, Morrison feels that he's got to top this last fanciful tale and so he gears up for the story of the evening. This one spins around a gunslinger named Martin (Scott Paulin) who is haunted by his murderous past.

All four stories are interesting in that they aren't necessarily classic horror. They most definitely have a *Twilight Zone*-type feeling to them, more focused on the drama and nastiness of the human psyche. They won't scare many *Twistern* fans, but they will thrill them.

The only film made by director Wayne Coe, he had the wisdom to allow Dourif and Jones to run with their characters. And boy, do they do a fantastic job! Their performances alone are worth the price of admission, simultaneously complex and fascinating. There's a lot of humor in the dialogue and the actors' portrayal of their characters. This is some classic old fashioned Western style yarn spinning, here.

Coe's previous credits are as the designer of a couple of movie posters. It's too bad that he's never made a follow-up. This would make a wonderful cable television series.

Saunter up to the campfire, warm yourself with a pull from your flask, and listen to some *Grim Prairie Tales*!

Morrison: "You city folk are a strange lot. You say, 'Shock me,' and then when I do, you say, 'Oh no, I didn't expect that!'"

JESSE JAMES MEETS FRANKENSTEIN'S DAUGHTER

(1965)

Directed by William Beaudine

Screenplay by Carl K. Hittlemen

Actors:

JOHN LUPTON
CAL BOLDER
NARDA ONYX
STEVEN GERAY
ESTELITA
RAYFORD BARNES
ROGER CREED
JIM DAVIS
DAN WHITE

Lightning crashes across the night sky, illuminating a Spanish monastery high on a hill. The village people run in fear, not because of the storm, but what evil occurrences are happening up in that now unholy place…

The next day, in a different tumbleweed town, there's a bare knuckle fight out in the street. Town folk surround the pugilistic display as two men bet on the outcome. One of those men is the legendary gunman Jesse James (John Lupton). James is rooting for the larger man, Hank Tracy (Cal Bolder), who happens to be his sidekick and friend.

Hank beats the other man down and the match is called in his favor. He and Jesse collect their money (with some difficulty), but it's clear that they are down on their luck and in need of more cash.

They pick up with a gang called The Wild Bunch. The gang has suffered lately, too, and their numbers are down to three, brothers Lonny and Butch (Rayford Barnes and Roger Creed) and their henchman, Pete (Dan White). Lonny has come up with a plan to rob a stagecoach full of cash and Butch brings Jesse and Hank on as hired guns, with an even split of the profits. Unfortunately, Lonny is a real snake in the grass and he double-crosses Jesse by telling the local lawman of their plans, with the hopes of collecting the bounty on James' head.

Things don't go well and Butch and Dan are gunned down in the firefight. Jesse whisks a wounded Hank away, with the posse hot on their trail.

Hank needs medical attention and when he and Jesse stumble across Juanita (Estelita), she suggests that they take Hank to the nearest doctor. Unfortunately, that turns out to be the inhabitants of the Spanish monastery, Maria (Narda Onyx) and Rudolph Frankenstein (Steven Geray). Despite the increasing reluctance of her brother, Maria is determined to carry on the disturbing reanimation experiments conducted by her grandfather.

Does Maria want to heal or kill Hank? Will Jesse catch on and stop her? Will the law catch up with Jesse?

Filmed in a grand total of eight days, *Jesse James Meets Frankenstein's Daughter* was released as a double feature with *Billy the Kid vs. Dracula,* a perfect *Twistern* duo.

This is most definitely an exploitation film in all its glory, displaying all the low-budget qualities that it can. Director William Beaudine was known in the industry as "One Shot" for his shooting style. While he also directed the aforementioned *Billy the Kid vs. Dracula,* he was responsible for hundreds of other movies and TV episodes. Film historians number his films somewhere around 350 to 500, a shocking number one way or the other. Beaudine's tactics for producing, promoting, and profiting from his films are legendary.

In the case of *Jesse James Meets Frankenstein's Daughter,* Narda Onyx's portrayal of Maria Frankenstein steals the show. Her performance is somewhat overshadowed by the cheap production, but it equals Colin Clive's iconic portrayal of Dr. Frankenstein in 1931's *Frankenstein.* Unfortunately, she's not provided with such classic lines as, "It's alive, it's alive!"

Instead, Dr. Maria Frankenstein says, "While you finish preparing, I shall activate the artificial brain."

You'll probably need an artificial brain to sit through this campy *Twistern,* but saddle up your zombie horse, break out the pitchforks, and settle in for this horror-Western that's tops in the cheese factor!

JONAH HEX

(2010)

Directed by Jimmy Hayward

Screenplay by Mark Neveldine and Brian Taylor

Actors:

JOSH BROLIN
JOHN MALKOVICH
MEGAN FOX
MICHAEL FASSBENDER
WILL ARNETT
TOM WOPATT
AIDAN QUINN

Panned by critics and some moviegoers, *Jonah Hex* appears on the surface to be just another big budget disaster. But in the *Twistern* genre, this psychedelic horror Western is nearly picture perfect.

Josh Brolin plays Jonah Hex, a man whose been stripped of everything he loves at the hand of the masochistic Confederate General Quentin Turnbull (John Malkovich). Jonah exacts his revenge and kills the General. Hideously scarred on half his face by Indians, Hex resorts to the only life he knows – killing other men. But now he is a killer for hire instead of a soldier, a job he excels at. When he finds out that Turnbull is still alive, he goes after him with a hellish vengeance.

All that would seem like pretty standard Western fare, but then things get interesting. Because Hex had been nursed back to health by Native Americans, he is able to temporarily revive the dead and find out what they know. And, although he is clearly mortal, his ability to withstand enormous physical damage has been heightened.

Hex is a pretty scary figure, but he's not the worst in this film. Some of the other characters are quite dark, including Turnbull's psychotic sidekick Burke (Michael Fassbender) and a mutant creature known only as "The Snake Man."

Brolin's portrayal of Hex is right on the money and this is possibly his best role yet. He's a gravelly voiced, physically damaged killing machine, yet he still has an ounce of humanity left in him (though perhaps just an ounce). His physical portrayal of this comic book-based character is spot on. Is it supposed to be realistic? No, his supernatural qualities remove any reference to that. But if you're able to go on the fantastical ride, you'll enjoy his performance.

One complaint about the movie is that Megan Fox, who plays a silly "prostitute with a heart of gold" character, is under-developed. The script doesn't give her much room to flesh out the role or even that much to do and she does the best she can with what she's got.

There are many horror movie elements present and the flashbacks are shown in prime psychedelic fashion. Again, this makes the movie stand out as a classic *Twistern*.

If you like comic book-based action movies featuring a rich guy with a bunch of gadgets dressed up like a bat, a whining dude in ridiculous spider web print tights, or a group of complainers with super powers they just don't want led by a bald guy in a wheel chair, you probably won't like this dusty, blasting, growling showdown of a movie. But, if your tastes runs more towards denizens of Hell with giant stone fists (*Hellboy*) and vigilantes set on bloody vendettas (*The Punisher*), this is one to add to your *Twistern* movie library.

Jonah Hex: "War and me took to each other real well. It felt like it had meaning. The feeling of doing what you thought was right. But it wasn't. Folks can believe what they like, but eventually a man's gotta decide if he's gonna do what's right. That choice cost me more than I bargained for."

LUST IN THE DUST

(1985)

Directed by Paul Bartel

Written by Philip John Taylor

Actors:
DIVINE
TAB HUNTER
GEOFFREY LEWIS
LAINIE KAZAN
HENRY SILVA
CESAR ROMERO
NEDRA VOLZ
COURTNEY GAINS
GINA GALLEGO

Rosie Velez (Divine) is a tramp seeking employment in the rough and tumble Old West town of Chile Verde, the home of ruffians and roustabouts. Before she even gets there, she runs afoul of Hard Case Williams (Geoffrey Lewis) and his gang. Fortunately, a handsome, silent stranger named Abel Wood (Tab Hunter) saves her.

But, there's trouble brewing and all of the characters that we meet have secondary reasons for occupying Chile Verde.

As the poster proclaimed, "He rode the West, the girls rode the rest!"

Divine must be the most well known transvestite in all of film history. Born Harris Glen Milstead, he defined and refined his character in some of the most noted "ultra bad taste" films, especially under the guidance of director and compatriot in riotous spectacles, John Waters. Together, they practically created the genre, forever changing film and art in the 1970s.

Unfortunately, *Lust in the Dust* does not have the fingerprints of Waters, but it might as well have. Almost all of his trademarks are present, and the film is better for it. Water was asked to direct but turned it down because he didn't write it.

Instead, the fantastic and equally creative Paul Bartel took the reins for this outrageous musical comedy *Twistern*. One of the brilliant and clever things about this movie is that it's always funny, but never played for laughs. As a result, it isn't cartoonish, and the viewer actually cares about the characters, the bad guys as well as the heroes.

The rest of the cast is rounded out by some truly great, underrated actors, especially Lainie Kazan, who plays Marguerita Ventura, the owner of the local watering hole. Cesar Romero even has a cameo role as Father Garcia, the padre that says, "Do not be afraid, my son. They will not shoot while I am beside you." When the villain states that he would be glad to put some holes in him with his six-shooter he squeaks, "I'll be in the church," turns, and runs.

There is a surprisingly sophisticated plot and it develops slowly, coming to a highly enjoyable conclusion without falling into a lot of the same, clichéd pitfalls that many standard Westerns do (comedy or otherwise).

This is meant to be R-rated adult entertainment and the jokes (spoken and visual) are raunchy. But, it's still pretty tame and won't spook most sophisticated ladies. This is a great one if you're looking for a rollicking, bawdy Western parody for grownups. This is the stuff great *Twisterns* are made of.

Narrator: "The legend of Chile Verde tells of men and women who became slaves to their passions. They paid the price here under the blistering, burning, blazing, scorching, roasting, toasting, baking, boiling, broiling, steaming, searing, sizzling, grilling, smoldering, VERY HOT New Mexico sun. For there is a saying in these parts: those who lust in the dust shall die in the dust."

NEAR DARK

(1987)

Directed by Kathryn Bigelow

Screenplay by Kathryn Bigelow and Eric Red

Actors:
ADRIAN PASDAR
LANCE HENRIKSEN
BILL PAXTON
JENNY WRIGHT
JENETTE GOLDSTEIN
JOSHUA JOHN MILLER
TOM THOMERSON
MARCIE LEEDS

Caleb Colton (Adrian Pasdar) is a bored young cowboy growing up in a sleepy Midwestern farming community who meets a fetching young lady named Mae (Jenny Wright) one evening. She seems a little distracted and keeps jawing about "the night." His hormones are pretty much locked on and he doesn't want to let her go home but she insists. Finally, he stops his truck and refuses to keep going without a kiss. With some abandon, she gives in and during the necking session, she gives him a nip on the neck that draws blood. Thus begins Caleb's journey into the world of a traveling clan of modern vampires, led by Jesse Hooker (Lance Henriksen), a vampire that was turned sometime during the Civil War.

The rest of the group consists of Diamondback, played by the versatile Jenette Goldstein, who also costarred in *Aliens* with Henriksen and Bill Paxton. Joshua John Miller is the child actor who plays Homer, the oldest vampire. Miller is the real life son of

Jason Patric, who also played a vampire in the movie *The Lost Boys,* released the same year.

Bill Paxton plays the most violent and humorous vampire, Severen. Unlike all of the other actors, Paxton overplays his character to the hilt, with fantastic results. Frankly, this movie would not be anywhere as entertaining as it is without his character. He delivers his dialogue with mucho gusto, sort of a psycho punk-rock cowboy wearing razor-sharp spurs and a leather jacket.

Kathryn Bigelow directed and co-wrote this modern tale of cowboy vampires. There are some strangely edited scenes, including some shots where the vampires drive their blacked-out RV into a warehouse for cover from the sun and the film has been sped up. It's as if Bigelow had to trim a second or two here and there to meet a required film length. While it's mildly distracting and makes the film seem a bit more dated than it actually is, it certainly doesn't ruin it.

The dialogue and the visuals are almost too clever at times and probably went right over the heads of the intended viewing demographics at the time. That doesn't mean that you won't appreciate the small details, though. Once again, these just add to an already interesting film.

The vampire myth itself is also fair game and in *Near Dark,* conventions are ignored and explored. For example, the vampires do not have pointy teeth in this movie. But, the extreme susceptibility to sunlight, the ability to create other vampires, and super strength are all incorporated. Interestingly, the film offers the possibility of reversing the process of becoming a vampire.

The amazing soundtrack is by the ever unique group, Tangerine Dream, which gives the film an absolutely surreal quality. This is another element that sets this film far apart from other vampire movies of the 1980s.

This was the final film released by the prodigious DeLaurentis Entertainment Group, which went out of business. As a result, there wasn't much, if any, marketing for this superb vampire Western. Don't you make the same mistake – see it! Just make sure you stay in the sunlight, Buckaroo…

Severen: "Howdy. I'm gonna separate your head from your shoulders. Hope you don't mind none."

NORTH STAR

(1996)

Directed by Nils Gaup

Screenplay by Gilles Behat, Sergio Donati and others

Actors:

JAMES CAAN
CHRISTOPHER LAMBERT
CATHERINE MCCORMACK
BURT YOUNG

Based on the book by Heck Allen, this is the story of a mad, power-crazed land baron named Sean McLennon (James Caan) who wants to steal all of the mining plots in his area of Alaska, including a sacred Indian cave. He's crazy for the gold and will kill to get his way!

A lone half-breed named Hudson Saanteek (Christopher Lambert) is the only man who stands in his way. McLennon sends his henchmen to wipe him out after Saanteek accidentally (is that possible?) kidnap his woman, Sarah (played by Catherine McCormack). The chase is on!

Okay, so that's not the most original plot on the prairie and it plays like a fairly typical Western. Where it becomes a *Twistern* is the setting is transposed to the arctic wasteland, with snow flurries replacing dust, fur instead of canvas long coats, and dog sleds instead of horses.

Christopher Lambert (who was also executive producer) as the half-breed Indian with lots of fake tan makeup just doesn't work. The man couldn't be more French and his accent is in full bloom here. It reminds this old cowpoke of the movies where they try to falsely convince us of racial authenticity using tons of makeup and surrounding them with more realistic looking actors. They don't call it a cattle call for no reason! Why couldn't they just make him a French trapper who was befriended by the Indians? I suppose that would have altered Allen's original story too much…

James Caan and Burt Young, two normally fantastic actors, moon around making extremely strange facial expressions as if they are auditioning for *The Phantom of the Opera.* Their performances are comical enough to watch this film just for the guffaws.

The fact that the *North Star* screenplay was co-written with legendary Western movie writer Sergio Donati (*Once Upon a Time in the West, For a Few Dollars More* and others) didn't seem to help. Ah, well.

Regardless, the scenery is fantastic. Reportedly shot in Norway, the snow is as much a character as any of the actors and you can practically feel the bone chilling cold.

Nils Gaup, the director has not been prolific over the years, but several of his other films are worth checking out, though they are not *Twisterns*. Maybe that's a good thing.

Still, this is a good hot summer Sunday afternoon movie to watch with a cold root beer in one hand and a Klondike bar in the other, dusty boots propped up on the footstool and your trusty dog by your side.

Sean McLennon: "Nobody dies till I say they die!"

OBLIVION

(1994)

Directed by Sam Irvin

Written by Charles Band

Actors:

ANDREW DIVOFF
RICHARD JOSEPH PAUL
GEORGE TAKEI
ISAAC HAYES
JULIE NEWMAR
RICHARD JOSEPH PAUL
JACKIE SWANSON
MEG FOSTER
CAREL STRUYCKEN
MUSETTA VANDER
JIMMIE F SKAGGS
IRWIN KEYES
JEFF MOLDOVAN

The concept of a *Twistern* may evoke the idea of a low-budget independent movie, with a crazy plot, nutty characterizations, and plenty of cheesy special effects. *Oblivion* has got to be one of the most perfect expressions of that vision, if not the poster child for the subgenre.

On a planet far away, an alien gunslinger named Redeye (Andrew Divoff) strides into the town of Oblivion and kills the sheriff. Redeye and his gang commence to shake up the town and cause general mayhem.

Meanwhile, the sheriff's estranged son, Zack Stone (Richard Joseph Paul), is out prospecting for a local ore named Dirconium that is wildly more valuable than gold and also interrupts electrical currents. Zack discovers a Native American warrior staked out for certain death at the claws of giant scorpions the size of a grizzly bear. He saves the poor soul, Buteo (Jimmie F. Skaggs), who tells him the story of how his family was brutally murdered.

Soon, the town mortician called Gaunt (Carel Struycken) shows up to inform Zack that his father has been gunned down by Redeye and the trio set off to Oblivion to see if they can help the hapless townsfolk.

The real delight here is the characters. Redeye's gang includes a Mongolian named Bork (Irwin Keyes), a flashy, knife-wielding caballero named Spanner (Jeff Moldovan), and a dominatrix named Lash (Musetta Vander) who carries an electrified whip. Redeye himself is a cape-wearing, gun-toting, lizard man with an eye patch sporting a giant red ruby.

It's not just the characters that are kooky, either. Oblivion is, on the surface, just another Old West tumbleweed town. But look closely, and you'll see that there are ATMs and outdoor ceiling fans that serve no purpose other than to further the ridiculous plot.

Can you tell that this movie has got to be a *Twistern* crown jewel? You betcha, Pardner!

There are a large number of Star Trek jokes. George Takei plays the town's dentist, barber, and robotics expert. He runs around spouting hilarious lines like, "Jim, beam me up!" as he downs a bottle of Jim Beam bourbon whiskey. He reportedly ad-libbed all of these classic lines and is clearly having a great time doing so. It's hard not to get caught up in the infectious fun.

Furthering the Star Trek connection, Meg Foster, who also appeared in *Star Trek: Deep Space Nine,* plays a robot deputy. Mussetta Vander, who plays Lash in *Oblivion,* appeared in *Star Trek: Voyager.*

The cast also includes such notable cultural icons as Julie Newmar and Isaac Hayes.

This is not a big-budget production, in any way shape or form. But, if you're in the mood for a true space Western that predates *Cowboys and Aliens* and doesn't take itself at all seriously, saddle up your rocket boots and ride!

Zack Stone: "I don't want to hurt anyone. But unfortunately, you happen to be standing right where my gun's about to go off."

OBLIVION 2: BACKLASH

(1996)

Directed by Sam Irvin
Written by Charles Band

Actors:
ANDREW DIVOFF
RICHARD JOSEPH PAUL
GEORGE TAKEI
ISAAC HAYES
JULIE NEWMAR
RICHARD JOSEPH PAUL
JACKIE SWANSON
MEG FOSTER
CAREL STRUYCKEN
MUSETTA VANDER
JIMMIE F SKAGGS
IRWIN KEYES
MAXWELL CAULFIELD

"It's high noon at the end of the universe!"

Shot sequentially with the original film but released a few years later, we follow all of the characters that we've grown to love. Or, is it that we're groaning, instead?

Who cares! Throw away all reality and jump boots first into the absurd world of *Oblivion 2: Backlash*!

The gang's all here and then some. A dandy bounty hunter by the name of Sweeney (Maxwell Caulfield) arrives to track down Lash (Musetta Vander), who is wanted for intergalactic crimes including espionage. But Lash doesn't want to go because she's just discovered a mine filled with Dirconium, the insanely valuable and desirable ore.

Meanwhile, Miss Kitty (Julie Newmar) is hiding a huge secret that she just can't quite spit out to Zack (Richard Joseph Paul). Zack is now the sheriff of Oblivion, replacing his deceased father. He's also courting Miss Mattie (Jackie Swanson), but he's floundering like a fish out of water.

About two-thirds of the way through the film, Andrew Divoff reappears as Jaggar, the brother of Redeye. But, he's not here to avenge the death of his brother (depicted in the first film). Instead, he's here to convince Lash to turn over the mine or take it from her by force. It's unclear how he knows Lash has the mine. The character is clearly a recycled Redeye complete with his makeup minus the eye patch but wearing a costume that looks like a mixture of a vampire's getup and Darth Vader's formal evening attire.

The absurdity from the first film is turned up another notch, although we miss the carnivorous fanged toad-thing and giant scorpions. This time around, we're rewarded with a horned, multi-nostril devil creature and a turtle the size of a mountain. Given how fast most turtles are and how they can just gnaw away at your ankles…it's not too scary, terrifying or even remotely unsettling.

Still, it's all great fun. Too bad George Takei seems to have run out of Star Trek jokes. His wide-eyed screeching is perfect, though. It would have been nice to see a third installment centered on his Doc Valentine character. Even better, how about a rollicking *Twistern* featuring his adventures with Mortician Gaunt (Carel Struycken) on his rocket powered funeral coach? That would be a downright hoot!

The majestic soundtrack is once again provided by The Bulgarian Orchestra, who did such a fine job with the first film. The special effects are not too bad for a low-budget production, especially the stop motion animation. Both *Oblivion* and *Oblivion 2* were reportedly made for $2.5 million each. The money seems to have been well spent.

The only thing that slows down *Oblivion 2: Backlash* is the editing of some of the scenes. It appears that there was some leeway given to the actors to allow them to deliver their lines in a leisurely fashion and this causes the pace to drag at times. Surely this could have been tightened up in editing.

But, once again, both *Oblivion* films stand as shining *Twistern* beacons in a sea of ho-hum big budget borefests. Whip yourself up a bowl of popcorn and discover the world that director Sam Irvin and crew have dreamt up.

OUTLAND

(1981)

Directed by Peter Hyams
Written by Peter Hyams

Actors:
SEAN CONNERY
PETER BOYLE
FRANCES STERNHAGEN
JAMES SIKKING
KIKA MARKHAM
CLARKE PETERS
STEVEN BERKOFF
JOHN RATZENBERGER

The plot of *Outland* is similar to the classic Western *High Noon.* And there, the *Twistern* connection pretty much ends. Yet, when the subject of sci-fi Westerns comes up, this movie is inevitably mentioned. In fact, it may be the prime example of the subgenre in the eyes of many folks.

It's a stretch because it follows the same groundwork laid by many a thriller, set in space or not. Still, because of the cult notoriety of the film, it should be included.

Federal Marshall William T. O'Niel (Sean Connery) is the new sheriff in a mining colony on one of the moons of Jupiter. Conditions are rough and Marshall O'Niel is warned by General Manager Mark Sheppard (Peter Boyle) that he expects a loose leash over his workers when it comes to their behavior. "My people work hard and they play hard," he declares.

But something is causing the miners to go crazy and commit extreme violence against themselves and others. Can the Marshall figure out what it is, and if so, can he stop it? Things come to an impasse when hired killers are sent to stop him in his quest.

Interestingly, *Outland* featured several ground-breaking new technologies that enhanced the production and viewers' experience. It was the first movie to use "Introvision," a special effect that allowed for combining the fore-, middle- and background in-camera. This allowed the actors to move around with and interact with the miniature sets instead of being in front of a green or blue screen. This effect is not that impressive nowadays, but it is still great fun to watch with a nostalgic eye.

It was also the debut of the "Megasound" sound system format, which allowed low-frequency sound effects to be projected from specific speakers, a precursor to the surround sound systems of today.

Outland is a slowly building thriller, like several other sci-fi films of the era. In terms of "feel," it has a fantastic similarity to such films as *Alien, Capricorn One* (which was also directed by Peter Hyams), *Silent Running, Logan's Run,* and *Saturn 3*. Real sci-fi buffs will be critical of the factual mistakes made, but again, this is all for entertainment sake, not scientific accuracy.

What really makes this film stand out is the stellar and highly acclaimed cast. Peter Boyle plays the boss with a fantastic darkness that contrasts superbly with Sean Connery's stoicism. Supporting roles are numerous and notable. Frances Sternhagen plays the salty colony doctor and she lays down funny lines like they're candy. James Sikking plays Montone, the Marshall's Sergeant who seems to be on the up and up. But what is his involvement and what does he know?

There are notable cameos by actors who were fairly unknown at the time. Steven Berkoff and a barely recognizable (he's in a space suit the entire scene) John Ratzenberger play miners who go crazy. Ratzenberger and Frances Sternhagen later worked together on the beloved TV comedy, *Cheers.* Berkoff came to widespread notoriety playing bad guys in such films as *Octopussy, Beverly Hills Cop* and *Rambo: First Blood Part II.*

I'll leave it to you to decide if this is truly a *Twistern,* but there is no doubt that this is a good, if not great, sci-fi action movie. Strap on your jet boots, grab your laser six shooter and head for that yonder moon, Cowboy!

RANGO

(2011)

Directed by Gore Verbinsky
Written by John Logan

Actors:
JOHNNY DEPP
ISLA FISHER
BILL NIGHY
ABIGAIL BRESLIN
ALFRED MOLINA
HARRY DEAN STANTON
RAY WINSTONE
NED BEATTY
TIMOTHY OLYPHANT

Where to start with the ways this movie is a *Twistern*…well, it's animated, for one! How many animated Westerns have there been? Not many! And this is a big-budget production, made for a measly $135 million. Okay, that ain't pocket change, but you get the picture!

Also, how about this for another crazy twist: there are very, very few humans in *Rango*. Instead, our hero is a pet chameleon who is accidentally stranded in the desert, far from his customary glass-enclosed world. He's not even a cowboy! Nope, it's just a persona that he displays to protect himself from the rough and ready denizens of this tumbleweed town. (He's a chameleon. Get it?)

Soon, it becomes clear that the town is dying from a lack of water and Rango is drafted to be the sheriff. Then all Hell breaks loose! Incidentally, that word pops up a distressing number of times. It's bandied about so often that it's disturbing. Maybe this old Cowpoke is a bit behind the times, but it just seems excessive.

For a movie that is obviously aimed at kids, it's perhaps more suited to an older audience. The movie features several psychedelic scenes that have obvious references to the infamous gonzo journalist, Hunter S. Thompson, as well as "spirit walks" where Rango sees "The Spirit of the West." Only a more adult audience would get all of the jokes and references, such as knowing that Johnny Depp, who voices Rango, starred in the film adaptation of Thompson's autobiographical novel, *Fear and Loathing in Las Vegas*. They would also understand "The Spirit of the West" is supposed to be Clint Eastwood (voiced by Timothy Olyphant).

Such things would not be understood by a little Dogie, but it all leads to great fun for us experienced ranch hands. The action and hilarity is pretty much non-stop, beginning with the chameleon travelling with the family that keeps him. A near-miss with a critter on the road causes his aquarium to launch out of the moving car and into the desert. A Don Quixote-type armadillo (Alfred Molina) points him in the direction of the town of Dirt, where he finally arrives after narrowly avoiding capture and consumption by a red-tailed hawk.

Par for the course, every big-budget animated movie ups the ante and *Rango* is no different. The CGI is simply stunning, including complex, realistic textures and ambient elements like dust. The soundtrack by noted composer Hans Zimmer is a mixture of mariachi music, atmospheric tracks, and manic chase pieces. Like all great soundtracks, it becomes an irreplaceable part of the goings on.

Rango is without a doubt, one of the finest animated *Twisterns* ever made.

Rango says, "Now, we ride!"

RAVENOUS

(1999)

Directed by Antonia Bird
Screenplay by Ted Griffin

Actors:
GUY PEARCE
ROBERT CARLYLE
DAVID ARQUETTE
JEREMY DAVIES
JEFFERY JONES
JOHN SPENCER
STEPHEN SPINELLA
NEAL MCDONOUGH

Lieutenant John Boyd (Guy Peirce) chooses to play dead while his unit is massacred around him by the Mexican Army. He ends up on the bottom of a cart piled high with his dead compatriots dripping blood in his face. With a sudden burst of bravery, he surprises and captures the Mexican commanding officers.

He is rewarded with the position of Captain, but it's clear that his achievement was because of his cowardice and he's lost his mind in the process. So, he's sent to the distant mountainous Fort Spencer to get him out the way and not bring any further embarrassment to the military.

It quickly becomes clear that the Fort is occupied by a group of undesirables – led by the oddball Colonel Hart (Jeffery Jones). Yet, when a half-starved man (Robert Carlyle) stumbles into the Fort with stories of a lost party of settlers who got stuck in a winter pass and had to result to cannibalism to survive, they set out to see if they can rescue anybody.

Things go from bad to worse.

There's quite a bit of gory, grisly action and disturbing insinuations. The plot is long-winded, with plenty of twists–maybe too many for some viewers. But, from within the pantheons of *Twistern* legend, it all makes for one of the finest horror drama thrillers ever made about Western-type characters.

There's an underlying theme of vegetarianism, which is not something you find in too many Westerns. Both Guy Pearce and director Antonia Bird are vegetarians in real life and this must have been a really interesting shoot in a lot of ways.

The cast as a whole is fantastic. Most of the supporting roles are so fully fleshed out (no pun intended) that it would be delicious (okay, that *was* intentional) to see them star in their own movies. But it's a real treat to watch two actors the caliber of Pearce and Carlyle work together. We can only hope it happens again in another project of this quality.

This was noted stage and screen actor John Spencer's last role. Many viewers will remember him from TV shows such as *The Patty Duke Show* and *The West Wing.*

Director Antonia Bird turned away from film after *Ravenous* and concentrated on television work. That's too bad, because there is a marvelously intriguing texture to the movie.

The writer, Ted Griffin, went on to create the excellent but short-lived television series *Terriers.*

The cinematography is spectacular, from claustrophobic interior shots to awesome landscapes that give an equally unsettling feeling.

Damon Albarn and Michael Nyman scored a perfect soundtrack for *Ravenous*. Albarn is a member of two alternative pop rock bands, *Blur* and *Gorillaz* (whose breakout hit was a song titled "Clint Eastwood"), while Nyman is a noted minimalist composer whose large body of work includes the soundtrack to the romantic sci-fi drama movie, *Gattaca.*

Throughout the film, the spirit of the old West shines through. If you can stomach it, *Ravenous* is finger licking good!

"If you die first, I am definitely going to eat you. But the question is, if I die, what are you going to do? Bon appétit! Eat or die," intones Colonel Ives.

RED HILL

(2010)

Directed by Patrick Hughes
Written by Patrick Hughes

Actors:
RYAN KWANTEN
STEVE BISLEY
TOMMY LEWIS
CLAIRE VAN DER BOOM
JIM DALY

A young police officer and his pregnant wife move to a sleepy burg named Red Hill in the Australian Outback. Right off the bat, we know that things ain't quite right. There's a big storm brewing. News reports are coming in that there's been an explosion at the maximum-security prison about six hours' drive away. And something – maybe a panther – attacked and killed a horse.

It's time to grab your gun, right? Wrong. Our shave tail hero actually forgets his sidearm as he leaves the house – he can't find it amongst all the boxes still to be unpacked.

So begins this quirky *Twistern* set in modern times. But, it's a world stuck in the Old Western idiom. People don't wear cowboy hats and boots as a fashion statement – that's just what they wear, sometimes it's just easier to ride a horse, and most folks are packing heat.

The all-Aussie cast is lead by the baby-faced Ryan Kwanten, best known for his role on the popular vampire television series, *True Blood.* His cantankerous boss at the police station is played by Steve Bisley, another well-known actor from the television show

Oz. Tommy Lewis plays the mysterious antagonist, a role that he also played in the movie *The Proposition*. His shadowy character is played with overtones of the horror movie genre to great effect.

Made for only $3 million, this is the first feature-length project from director Patrick Hughes, who also wrote, produced, and edited it. He's one to watch. His touch is picture perfect, a real homage to some of the best Westerns but with plenty of modern and unique twists, especially how the action and thriller elements are ramped up. *Red Hill* is pure Western, but also a bit outside the genre. A similar feeling movie is the Coen Brothers' movie *No Country For Old Men*, then add a dash of *Halloween* stalker-slasher, and you've got yourself a really interesting blend of Western, horror, thriller, action, drama, and psychedelic.

The knockout Western soundtrack by Dmitri Golovko, the stunning scenery shot in Omeo, Victoria, and the superb script make for a superb film.

It's too bad that this film didn't receive more marketing in this country. There are plenty of folks that would have really enjoyed it. If you're reading this book, I know you will!

RED SUN

(1971)

Directed by Terence Young
Written by Laird Koenig, Denne Bart Petitclerc

Actors:
CHARLES BRONSON
TOSHIRO MIFUNE
URSULA ANDRESS
ALAIN DELON

A train robbery is in the cards for Link Stuart (Charles Bronson) and his outlaw gang of thieves and bandits. But, when his right hand man, Guache (Alain Delon), tries to murder him during a successful job, the tables are turned and Link becomes a victim.

Guache makes off with a ceremonial Japanese sword that was being delivered to the President of the United States as a gift. After the train robbery, a samurai named Kuroda Jubei (Toshiro Mifune) is given the job of tracking down the sword and killing Guache. He has two stipulations; he must take Stuart with him to act as a guide and he has one week to complete the task or he must commit ritualistic suicide.

While both Kuroda and Stuart are warriors, they live by different moral codes of honor. Stuart grows to appreciate Kuroda's samurai way as they track down Guache's girlfriend, Cristina (Ursulla Andress), who can lead them to the gang.

Red Sun has a dated, yet polished feel to it. The international cast does a fantastic job and the Spanish scenery is stunning. What sets *Red Sun* apart as a *Twistern* is the Japanese culture meets the Old West, of course. And you couldn't find two better actors in their prime to weave this story. Charles Bronson previously starred in *The Magnificent Seven,* which was a remake of *Seven Samurai,* which starred Toshiro Mifune. This is the only film in which both actors appeared together and the results are superb.

Based on a true story, director Terence Young paints an exciting picture. Young is primarily known for several excellent thrillers and numerous James Bond films. While primarily television writers, Laird Koenig and Denne Bart Petitclerc do a fine job creating a vision of this clash of cultures.

The chance to see Mifune and Bronson act together is worth the price of admission alone. *Red Sun* is well worth a couple of days' hard ride to see. So saddle up and don't forget your kimono.

The movie poster tagline declared, "2 Desperados ... 1 Hellcat ... and a Samurai ... the greatest fighting force the West has ever known!"

RENEGADE

(2004)

Directed by Jan Kounen
Screenplay by Jean-Michel Charlier

Actors:
VINCENT CASSEL
JULIETTE LEWIS
MICHAEL MADSEN
ERNEST BORGNINE
DJIMON HOUNSOU
GEOFFREY LEWIS
HUGH O'CONOR
EDDIE IZZARD
TEMUERA MORRISON
COLM MEANEY
KATERI WALKER
KESTENBETSA

Also released under the title *Blueberry*, this French film is a live-action version of graphic novel artist Jean "Moebius" Giraud's unique vision. Brought to the screen by director Jan Kounen and adapted as a screenplay by Jean-Michel Charlier, this story follows a young man named Mike Donovan (Vincent Cassel).

Mike is sent out West to live with his uncle, who is supposed to toughen him up and teach him the ways of the world. But, his uncle is a drunk and his method of education involves using an iron fist and Mike rebels.

One night, Mike steals money from his uncle and sneaks out to visit a prostitute. During his amorous encounter, an evil gunfighter named Wallace Blount (Michael Madsen) bursts into the room and threatens the prostitute. Things go horribly wrong and the woman is killed, the brothel goes up in flames, and Mike barely escapes with a bullet in his shoulder.

In his delirium, he wanders into the desert, where he collapses. A kindly Indian finds him and takes him back to his village set in the rocky cliffs. There, he is introduced to a new kind of living and heals physically, if not spiritually. He also discovers that the Indians are hiding something that the world at large must never know about.

Mike grows up and becomes a U.S Marshall. He also protects the Indians and the secret buried in the sacred mountains.

A German prospector named Prosit (Eddie Izzard) believes that there's gold in the region and, using a blood-stained manuscript, pursues the treasure. The unscrupulous Prosit will sacrifice everything and everyone in his secretive search, including his friends. His compatriout, Woodhead (Djimon Hounsou), and his employer, ranch boss Greg Sullivan (Geoffrey Lewis), fall victim to his greed.

Meanwhile, Sullivan's beautiful daughter Maria (Juliet Lewis) has a secret of her own – she's in love with Mike.

When Mike's nemesis Blount reappears and starts causing havoc, you know we're in for an epic battle. Will Mike heal the hole in his spirit or will Wallace gun him down first? Will Maria's love go unrequited? Will Prosit find the treasure, and what *is* it, exactly? Is it gold, jewels, or something else entirely?

Stunningly filmed by cinematographer Tetsuo Nagata, *Renegade* is a real mind trip. Employing computer generated psychedelic images, the characters drink an Indian sacramental concoction that allows them to leave the physical plane and examine their true inner selves.

Renegade was released on DVD and never played on US theater screens. Marketed as a standard Western, it's far from it. While there are classic Western cues, it's the portrayal of shamanic experiences that make this a superb *Twistern.*

Don't miss director Jan Kounen's cameo as Billy, the mentally handicapped son of lawman Rolling Star (Ernest Borgnine) and Colm Meaney as Jimmy McClure, Mike's right hand man.

The cast is superb and the actors add tremendous depth to every role, big or small.

"Animals are beasts, but men are monsters," growls Wallace Blount.

Don't miss this prime psychedelic *Twistern*!

RUSTLER'S RHAPSODY

(1985)

Directed by Hugh Wilson
Written by Hugh Wilson

Actors:
TOM BERENGER
G.W. BAILEY
ANDY GRIFFITH
FERNANDO REY
SELA WARD
MARILU HENNER
JIM CARTER

In *Rustler's Rhapsody,* Tom Berenger is one of those rare actors that can easily blend humor and the pathos of an action hero. For this clever comedy, he plays Rex O'Herlihan, the singing cowboy, who rides into town to save the day. Berenger's character is fully aware of his role in the plot and what the future will hold, all with truly hilarious results.

G.W. Bailey plays the town drunk, Peter, who decides to be the sidekick, much to Rex's displeasure. Rex has never had a sidekick, preferring to do his job alone, and doesn't want Peter to get hurt. Bailey's characterization of Peter is spot on in every detail. His masterful recreation of the classic Western sidekick is fun to watch. Bailey is best known for his manic tough-guy roles in such slapstick comedy classics as the *Police Academy* (which Hugh Wilson also directed and wrote the screenplay for) series and *M*A*S*H.* Originally cutting his teeth in television, he had roles in *Charlie's Angels* and *Starsky and Hutch.* He was also an integral part of the cast of the excellent crime drama, *The Closer*.

The bad guy is interestingly played by the seminal good guy, Andy Griffith. Griffith is impossible to revile as the evil cattle baron and, fortunately, they don't make him irreversibly evil. That may sound like it doesn't make for a good foil for Berenger's hero, but it really works.

The movie also has another bad guy, a railroad baron (two barons for the price of one!) played by the superb Spanish actor Fernando Rey. But his character is unnecessary, underutilized, and easily discarded here.

Sela Ward and Marilu Henner are sadly relegated to the status of eye candy. Both are such wonderful actors, and while they have some great lines and character quirks, they are also underutilized. Ward plays the headstrong daughter of the railroad baron, and Henner plays the purposefully stereotypical prostitute with a heart of gold.

Jim Carter, an actor that you might recognize but who rarely plays the lead, has a fun cameo as Blackie the cattle baron's henchman. He's so evil that the script calls for his removal as quickly as possible.

Blackie's treatment and swift exit illustrate perfectly what is going on with this film. It examines and pokes fun at the Western stereotypes with a genuine love for the genre. You know exactly what is going to happen when the two barons set out to kill Rex by hiring another good guy gunslinger. The characters, the script, and everything about this movie are self aware from a completely modern perspective.

Some of the humor is in the same vein as other similar comedies of the 70s and 80s, poking fun at questions of sexuality. Some viewers might find those kinds of laughs rather dated and maybe even a bit tasteless.

The production values are superb. The soundtrack is marvelous, and the cinematography perfect. Being from the mid 80s, the editing is a bit slower than modern audiences are used to and the camera occasionally hangs on the actors a bit too long.

But in *Rustler's Rhapsody* it's not about the destination, but the journey in this genuinely funny *Twistern.*

"Give me a tall glass of warm gin with a human hair in it," drawls Rex O'Herlihan.

SERENITY

(2005)

Directed by Joss Whedon
Written by Joss Whedon

Actors:
NATHAN FILLION
GINA TORRES
ALAN TUDYK
MORENA BACCARIN
ADAM BALDWIN
JEWEL STAITE
SEAN MAHER
SUMMER GLAU
RON GLASS
CHIWETEL EJIOFOR
DAVID KRUMHOLTZ

Captain Malcolm "Mal" Reynolds (Nathan Fillion) is a simple guy. He just wants to keep flying and make a reasonable living for himself and his crew. But the evil government, The Alliance, makes it harder and harder to find honest, independent work. And his two fugitive passengers, brother and sister duo Simon and River Tam (Sean Maher and Summer Glau), make it even harder. So if he has to resort to thieving and crime, well, those are the choices a man has to make. And if he has to shoot somebody in the process, well, he's prepared to do that too.

His ship, Serenity, is a Firefly-class transport spaceship that has seen better days and more than its share of adventure. It makes the *Millennium Falcon* look like a luxury liner.

When the crew is attacked by cannibals known as Reavers during a job, Simon decides to protect River from further involvement in dangerous escapades by leaving the ship. But before he can whisk her safely away, she randomly attacks the patrons of a bar, almost killing Mal and his right hand man, Jayne Cobb (Adam Baldwin), in the process. With The Alliance hot on their heels and the constant threat of Reaver attacks, Mal must figure out the secret River's been carrying around before it gets them all killed.

A continuation of the cult classic TV series, *Firefly*, the movie picks up where the show left off. It's not necessary to see the original television show to enjoy *Serenity*, but it will give the viewer a much fuller, more satisfying experience. New viewers won't know the difference and will be immediately sucked into the unique galaxy created by Joss Whedon, while fanatics will be glad to see their old friends on the big screen.

Many of the plot elements are familiar, but are presented in a unique and interesting way. For example, our heroes battle not one, but two enemies. The Alliance is completely ordered and logical in its actions. The Reavers are absolutely the opposite: chaotic, unpredictable, and driven by raw rage and hunger. Both are nearly insurmountable foes for our lovable, rag-tag crew, and ample evidence of just one aspect of Whedon's brilliant writing. This is not a simple story. Instead, there are multiple, interwoven story threads that reward the highly attentive and observant viewer.

Filmed on a relatively shoestring budget, largely due to the demands and support of the rabid fan base known as Browncoats, *Serenity* unfortunately did not make a large profit. Possibly Joss Whedon's best work to date (debatable if you are fan of his other works), there is no doubt that this is one of the all-time best

Twisterns set in space. Put it on the top of your list of must-see movies, if you haven't had the pleasure.

"Take my love, take my land
Take me where I cannot stand
I don't care, I'm still free
You can't take the sky from me
Take me out to the black
Tell 'em I ain't comin' back
Burn the land and boil the sea
You can't take the sky from me
There's no place I can be
Since I found serenity
But you can't take the sky from me"
- Firefly Theme Song, written by Joss Whedon

STINGRAY SAM

(2009)

Directed by Cory McAbee
Written by Cory McAbee

Actors:
CORY MCABEE
CRUGIE
DAVID HYDE PEIRCE
JOSHUA TAYLOR
WILLA VY MCABEE

Stingray Sam (Cory McAbee) is working as a lounge singer and bouncer at a sleazy bar when his old pal The Quasar Kid (Crugie) saunters in. Delighted to see each other after such a long absence, they happily engage in a "secret" handshake which involves thumb wrestling, fist bumps, and slaps to the face for several minutes.

Finally, The Quasar Kid tells Sam where he's been and that he's in trouble. Seems that he needs to do a job or he'll be in even deeper trouble. Stingray Sam is doubtful he can help his friend, but the choice is taken away from him when The Quasar Kid knocks him out and kidnaps him!

The job turns out to be rescuing a little girl. In the future, due to medical advances and a twisted society, men have the ability to give birth and determine the sex of every newborn baby. The choice is invariably male, so this little girl is a rare person indeed.

Will Sam and The Quasar Kid be able to rescue her? Or, will they fail at their attempt? Find out in *Stingray Sam*!

Presented as six episodes in the style of the *Flash Gordon* serial from the 1930s, *Stingray Sam* is narrated by David Hyde Pierce. This is a mix of Western, science fiction, and minimalist comedy, punctuated by musical numbers and illustrated by collages reminiscent of Terry Gilliam's work in Monty Python.

Shot in black and white, with simple but effective sets, the entire production was created with the idea that it could be viewed on a variety of devices, from a movie theater screen down to a handheld device such as a cell phone. This ambitious project was created with a tiny budget and did not involve a major production house. Still, the quality is rather high, and there have been some comparisons to Richard Elman's whacky 1982 cult classic, *Forbidden Zone.*

Stingray Sam does an amazing job of creating an interesting ambience and characters, all while mixing movie genres with abandon to humorous results. It will be jarring for some viewers when confronted by the less than stellar acting and cheap special effects. But, if you just let some of the cattle out of the barn of your mind and settle in to enjoy *Stingray Sam* in the spirit it was intended, you're in for an enjoyable hour.

Make sure you have a handful of olives ready for The Quasar Kid!

STRAIGHT TO HELL

(1987)

Directed by Alex Cox

Screenplay by Alex Cox and Dick Rude

Actors:

SY RICHARDSON
JOE STRUMMER
DICK RUDE
COURTNEY LOVE
JENNIFER BALGOBIN
BIFF YEAGER
PETER STACY
XANDER BERKELEY
GRACE JONES
DENNIS HOPPER
ELVIS COSTELLO
MIGUEL SANDOVAL

A fascination with punk rock culture inspired auteur filmmaker Alex Cox to shoot a concert film in Nicaragua featuring *The Clash* and several other bands. When that fell through, it was decided to use the money that was raised to make a movie, instead. Collaborators Dick Rude and Cox obtained permission to rewrite Guilio Questi's 1967 Spaghetti Western classic *Django, Kill!,* which they did using their own particular talents. What emerged was *Straight To Hell,* an absurdist homage featuring senseless violence, high sexual energy, and highlighting a unique cast.

Four bank robbers go on the lam and hole up in a deserted tumbleweed town when their stolen car breaks down. Norwood (Sy Richardson) is the cold-blooded leader of the gang. He oozes the calm, cool, killer vibe of a very dangerous desert snake, while his underage and pregnant wife, Velma (Courtney Love), demands the trappings of the high life in a piercing, screeching voice. But, it's the constantly angry Willy (Dick Rude) and the super slick Sims (Joe Strummer) that really steals the show. Their characters are haphazard, chaotic, frightening, and hilarious.

Unfortunately, the town is actually inhabited by a gang of roughnecks that dress up like caballeros, like to shoot anything that moves, and are more than a little addicted to coffee. They end up accepting Norwood and the gang and coexist in a chaotic tableau.

There are a lot of subplots, some of which don't go anywhere, but they are all interesting and the dialogue is genius, a mix of crime, Western, and street talk spoken with various accents.

Don't miss cameos by Jim Jarmusch, Peter "Spider" Stacy, Miguel Sandoval, Dennis Hopper, Xander Berkeley, Grace Jones, and Elvis Costello. If you're a fan of Alex Cox movies, you'll recognize many of the same actors. Watching this cast interact with each other is worth the price of admission alone.

Straight To Hell was not received well by most critics and many (including Cox himself) have felt that the film had a lot of room for improvement, given more time and budget. Upset by her portrayal, Courtney Love allegedly walked out of the premiere. Still, despite the negativity surrounding the picture, it is a *Twistern* classic. The action is engrossing, the dust is so real you'll choke, the characters are brilliant in their campy genius and the end result is a cerebrally interactive experience.

In 2010, Cox was inspired by Francis Ford Coppola's *Apocalypse Now Redux* and a director's cut titled *Straight To Hell Returns* appeared (and then promptly disappeared again) with additional scenes, enhanced FX, and a cleaned up print. While not hugely superior to the original, it's worthwhile lassoing this version for viewing. Some fans have hailed this as an all-time cult classic and every viewer will most definitely come away from this film with a firm opinion.

Prepare for surreal kookiness and be in a punk rock mood…

"Synchronize your watches… ten o'clock," commands Norwood.

"10:30," replies Willy.

Sims adds, "One minute to nine."

"Close enough," declares Norwood.

SUKIYAKI WESTERN DJANGO

(2007)

Directed by Takashi Miike
Written by Takashi Miike and Masa Nakamura

Actors:
QUENTIN TARANTINO
HIDEAKI ITO
MASANOBU ANDO
KOICHI SATO
KAORI MOMOI
YUSUKE ISEYA
RENJI ISHIBASHI
YOSHINO KIMURA
TERUYUKI KAGAWA

Prolific Japanese cult film director Takashi Miike brings us the brutal samurai *Twistern*, 2007's *Sukiyaki Western Django.*

The film opens with a dead man, a bullet hole through his head. When a hawk grabs a snake slithering by the body and flies off with it, a mysterious cowboy named Piringo (Quentin Tarantino) shoots it out of the sky, cuts it open and removes an egg, which he plans to fry and eat. But before he can, a trio of bad guys ride up, intent on killing him. Piringo stalls by entertaining them (in a bizarre Japanese accent) with the tale of two rival clans, who have overtaken a town in search of buried treasure.

Piringo spins a yarn about a mysterious gunfighter (Hideaki Ito) who rides into the town of Yuta (located in "Nevata") and offers his six-gun talents to the highest paying crew. Of the two clans, the Genji are stronger and have been forcing the weaker Heiki to search for the loot, but both believe that the gunman will sway their odds and make them dominant.

The plot thickens when it becomes clear that the gunman isn't interested in money or even chosing a gang to side with. Instead, he is there to help the prostitute Shizuka (Yoshino Kimura) seek revenge on the two groups, who were responsible for the murder of her husband and other atrocities.

Sukiyaki Western Django is a retelling of the classic Hatfield-McCoy story, which was inspired by William Shakespeare's *Romeo and Juliet*. There are numerous references to the Japanese Genpai War (1180-1185) as well as the English War of the Roses (1455-1485). Cinematic references to Akira Kurosawa's *Yojimbo* and Sergio Corbucci's *Django* are also present.

Mixing Western elements with chambara (samurai cinema), unique characteristics in the film include forcing the Japanese-speaking cast to speak English in an Old West accent, which created the need for subtitles. The plot is intriguing and engrossing enough that we're quickly pulled into the story despite all of the eccentricity. The acting is excellent, if intentionally a bit one-dimensional and the cinematography is hands down gorgeous. Don't miss Teruyuki Kagawa as the sheriff with multiple personalities and the steampunk elements such as a wooden power wheelchair.

Generally panned by critics, *Twistern* fans are going to love *Sukiyaki Western Django.* This is a true homage to the Western genre, but seen through the eyes of a samurai. Be ready to wield a sword in one hand and your six-gun in the other.

"The sound of the Gion Shoja temple bells echoes the impermanence of all things. The color of the sala flowers reveals the truth that to flourish is to fall. The proud do not endure, like a passing dream on a night in spring. The mighty fall at last…to be no more than dust before the wind," declares Piringo ominously.

SUNDOWN: THE VAMPIRE IN RETREAT

(1990)

Directed by Anthony Hickox
Written by Anthony Hickox and John Burgess

Actors:
DAVID CARRADINE
JIM METZLER
MORGAN BRITTANY
BRUCE CAMPBELL
MAXWELL CAULFIELD
DEBORAH FOREMAN
M EMMET WALSH
DANA ASHBROOK
JOHN IRELAND

A dominant bloodsucker named Jozek Mardulak (David Carradine) decides to lead a group of like-minded fanged friends to a deserted Old West town, where they establish a retiring lifestyle. Instead of hunting human victims for sustenance, they try developing a synthetic blood substitute. The problem is, they can't seem to perfect the process, so they seek the assistance of a human that has ties to one of their own.

David Harrison (the underrated Jim Metzler) has a beautiful wife and two young daughters. In his college years, he had a nemesis named Shane (Maxwell Caulfield) who almost stole his wife away. But Shane wants to bury the hatchet and invites him to come to Purgatory to consult at the blood substitute manufacturing facility. So, the kids are packed up and they hit the road for a two-week working vacation in the desert. Little do they know that Purgatory is full of thirsty vampires.

There are a couple of subplots going on, including the youthful relative of Abraham van Helsing the vampire hunter (Bruce Campbell), who has tracked Mardulak to Purgatory. The subplots don't really add much to the storyline, but don't distract from it, either.

One great aspect of *Sundown: The Vampire in Retreat* is the character development. These are not one-dimensional creations. Instead, they are precisely who they should be – the simpler ones do dumb things and the brighter ones figure stuff out. For example, a scientific, enterprising vampire figures out how to make hardwood-tipped bullets. Instead of a stake driven through the heart, imagine the damage wrecked by an automatic machine gun with its cartridge loaded with those bad boys! But you still have to pierce the heart.

Another interesting twist is the ability of the Purgatory vampires to be out in daylight. Instead of igniting in an instant blaze, they slather on sunblock, don dark glasses, gloves, and a big hat; and they're ready to go!

Several notable actors make appearances and it's a lot of fun to see them ham it up for the cameras, including M. Emmet Walsh (*Blade Runner, Blood Simple, Raising Arizona*), Dana Ashbrook (*Twin Peaks*), Morgan Brittany (*Dallas*), Deborah Foreman (*Valley Girl, My Chauffeur, April Fool's Day, Real Genius, Waxwork*), and several other faces that you might recognize. They all have fun roles and they make the most of what little screen time they have.

The music is a mixture of great tunes from the 50s and a superb original Western themed soundtrack by Richard Stone, a soundtrack composer for cartoons. So, there's a real lightness injected into the shadows of the typically dark vampire genre here, which is refreshing.

This Western horror/comedy was never released in theaters because the distribution house, Vestron Pictures, went out of business. (Doesn't that just...suck?!?) That's too bad because it would have made a great mid-summer release. Fortunately, it's since been released on DVD to an appreciative cult following.

This movie is a definite part of the *Twisted* Western genre, even though there are only token classic Western elements (the tumbleweed town, the geographical setting, the showdown, horses and costuming). This cult gem is better than you'd expect and worth staking a claim on the couch with a bowl of popcorn.

The tagline for the movie read, "There are two kinds of folks in Purgatory; vampires and lunch!"

TEARS OF THE BLACK TIGER

(2000)

Directed by Wisit Sasanatieng
Written by Wisit Sasanatieng

Actors:
CHARTCHAI NGAMSAN
STELLA MALUCCHI
SUPARKORN KISUWON
SUWINIT PANJAMAWAT
ARAWAT RUANGVUTH
SOMBAT METANEE

Gather round the campfire for a melodramatic *Twistern* from Thailand.

Dum (Chartchai Ngamsan) is a member of the outlaw gang known as The Black Tigers. He's in love with a young woman named Rampoey (Stella Malucchi) who, unfortunately, is betrothed to another. Will they come together, or does fate have other plans for them?

This is a fascinating look at how another culture views Westerns. While all of the elements are present, they're combined with the unexpected. Over-saturated colors make them really pop on screen, adding a surreal quality, almost as if we're watching an animated feature. Cowboys wear stylized clothing, packing pistols in a shoulder holster instead of the typical thigh carry. They just as easily wield a fully automatic machine gun as a standard Winchester lever-action rifle.

Despite some fast-paced action scenes, this is a fairly slow paced yarn about tragic romance. In addition to all of the stunning visuals, there are interesting plot twists involving betrayal and tests of loyalty.

Tears of the Black Tiger was the directorial debut for Wisit Sasanatieng, whose previous credits are as a screenplay writer. He does a spectacular job here, bringing something truly new and different to the Western genre.

Many of the scenes are shot on location, and there's one uniquely shot on a stage in front of a painted, impressionistic backdrop. This gives the film an almost two dimensional quality, like a viewing a living painting.

The bloodshed is surprisingly visceral. Not only is there a spray of hemoglobin, but chunks of flesh go flying when the bullets fly. That might be problematic if you watch *Tears of the Black Tiger* with someone else who enjoys the love story, but is repulsed by the bloodshed.

The cast is excellent, especially Malucchi, who has a real classic 50s look and way to her, Ngamsan who oozes charisma as a perfect leading man, and Suparkorn Kitsuwon, who plays Dum's bizarre sidekick. Kitsuwon practically steals the show with his evil arched eyebrow and pencil thin mustache.

In native Thai, the title is *Fah talai jone,* which roughly conveys "obsolescence, the feel of great chic or predestination." A combination of fashion, Western and foreign culture make this a distinctive *Twistern.*

Sadly, Miramax acquired the US distribution rights and attempted to edit the running time of the film. After less than satisfactory results, they shelved the film until Magnolia Pictures acquired the rights. Magnolia promptly released it on DVD, and it has gained critical and cult success in the original, uncut form.

There have been a surprising number of Westerns from Thailand. Hopefully, *Tears of the Black Tiger* signals a resurgence of the genre from the Land of Smiles.

"By everything sacred in this world, I, Mahesuan, swear, with the Buddha as my witness, I'll always be true and loyal to my blood brother, Dom, the Black Tiger who saved my life. If I break this oath, may his gun take my life," pledges Mahesuan.

Don't miss this marvelous movie. As the poster tagline read; "How the West was won… in the East!"

THE APPLE DUMPLING GANG

(1975)

Directed by Norman Tokar
Screenplay by Don Tait

Actors:
TIM CONWAY
DON KNOTTS
BILL BIXBY
SUSAN CLARK
SLIM PICKENS
HARRY MORGAN
JOHN MCGIVER

Based on the Jack Bickham novel by the same name, this *Twistern* is the story of a gambler (Bill Bixby) who winds up taking charge of three orphans. The children find gold, but make the mistake of trusting two bumbling idiots (the comedy genius duo Tim Conway and Don Knotts), who proceed to mess everything up to hilarious results.

Conway and Knotts play Amos Tucker and Theodore Ogelvie, respectively. The plot, while certainly serviceable and most definitely entertaining, takes a second seat to the performances of two of the finest comedians ever to see the silver screen. While Theodore is the smart one in comparison to thick as a brick Amos, that doesn't mean either will be receiving invites to the next MENSA meeting. Yet, neither actor makes their characters so moronic that they are unlikeable or unappealing, which happens with over the top slapstick characters. All credit goes to the skillful acting and masterful portrayal by the real stars of *The Apple Dumpling Gang.* Both actors went on to co-star together in several other comedies, including *The Prize Fighter* and *The Private Eyes*.

Bill Bixby is hugely enjoyable as card shark Russell Donovan and the rest of the cast is made up of several notable actors who clearly have great fun with their roles. Susan Clark co-stars as Magnolia Dusty Clydesdale, a stagecoach driver who marries Donovan so they can get custody of the orphans. Slim Pickens, Harry Morgan, and John McGiver also appear. Morgan plays Sheriff McCoy, who also happens to be the town barber and judge.

Buddy Baker composed the cheerfully fantastic music, just as he did for many Disney productions, while folk musician Randy Sparks and his band, The Back Porch Majority, perform the theme song.

Norman Tokar, noted director of TV and film, created this classic Disney movie for adult and juvenile cowpokes of all ages. You can't go wrong with any production with Tokar's name attached to it. The sequel, *The Apple Dumpling Gang Rides Again*, was not directed by Tokar. While it was not as well received by critics and it did not perform as well at the box office, it's equally hilarious and wonderful to see Knotts and Conway continuing in the roles of Amos and Theodore.

The Apple Dumpling Gang became the biggest box office hit of the 1970s for Disney. It also holds the honor of being the first Disney film released on videocassette.

In the list of classic *Twisterns*, a movie like *Blazing Saddles* would be at the top of the list in adult comedies. *The Apple Dumpling*

Gang would be right there alongside it, but this is one that the whole family can easily enjoy!

Amos: "How much money do you figure that dude's got in front of him?"

Theodore: "About five hundred."

Amos: "Five hundred? Wow! You know, that'll be, uh, that's two hundred apiece!"

THE BURROWERS

(2008)

Directed by J.T. Petty
Written by J.T. Petty

Actors:
CLANCY BROWN
WILLIAM MAPOTHER
KARL GEARY
SEAN PATRICK THOMAS
DOUG HUTCHINSON
JOCELIN DONAHUE
GALIN HUTCHINSON
LAURA LEIGHTON

It's a bright, sunny day and there's a slight breeze that rustles the tall grass in the open fields. But, there's also a faint, strange noise deep in the shadows of the trees and a shiver runs down your spine…

Have you ever had that feeling? How about the feeling that something or someone is watching you from just inside the edge of a dark forest? That's pretty creepy!

The Burrowers plays on those fears much as *Jaws* made a generation hesitant to dip a toe into a suburban pool. Like other classic horror films that don't immediately reveal the monster right away, this horror Western does a good job of letting your imagination get the best of you.

It's the late 1800s in the Dakota Territory and a posse is dispatched to find some kidnapped settlers. Their homes were attacked and most of the people massacred, except a select few. Why and where are the ones that were taken?

This is a well done film by horror director J.T. Petty and stars a hugely capable cast. There is no lead actor. Instead, the focus jumps from character to character. This results in a well developed ensemble effort.

The posse is made up of John Clay (Clancy Brown), the grizzled leader bent on getting the job done, his second in charge; William Parcher (William Mapother), an Indian fighter who has a real respect for his former adversaries; Fergus Coffey (Karl Geary), an Irish immigrant determined to get his kidnapped fiancée back; and cowboy Walnut Callaghan (Sean Patrick Thomas), a freed slave.

On their quest to rescue the kidnapped folks, they run across Captain Henry Victor (Doug Hutchinson), a psychotic, racist US Cavalry officer. Victor doesn't care what really happens; he just wants to kill every Indian he comes across. If anyone else gets in his way, black or white, he's not opposed to killing them, too.

The Burrowers is a well made independent film that was never released in the theaters. It's a downright shame that this film went straight to DVD. The moody, overcast prairie scenes surely would have been spectacular on the big screen.

The slower pace of the beginning really builds suspense and by the time you get to the actual critters, you've spooked yourself out pretty darn good. This isn't a particularly gory film, but there is plenty of violence and the special effects are better than the typical made-for-TV or direct-to-DVD movie.

The original music by composer Joseph LoDuca ties everything together, adding creepiness to the wide, expansive cinematography.

If you're looking for more monsters (and not the human kind) in your Western, this is one not to miss. Saddle up and keep your eyes on the ground!

"You'll be awake in your grave. You'll be alive when they feed."

Don't miss it!

THE GOOD, THE BAD, THE WEIRD

(2008)

Directed by Kim Jee-woon
Written by Kim Jee-woon

Actors:
LEE BYUNG-HUN
JUNG WOO-SUNG
SONG KANG-HO
YOON JE-MOON
RYOO SEUNG-SOO
SONG YEONG-CHANG
SON BYEONG-HO
OH DAL-SU
UHM JI-WON

Director Kim Jee-woon billed his *The Good, The Bad, The Weird* as "a kimchee Western." Kimchee is the spicy, vibrant red and white Korean dish made of fermented cabbage, and that aptly describes this wild homage to Sergio Leone's *The Good, The Bad and The Ugly.*

The scene is set when Park "The Bad" Chang-yi (Lee Byung-hun) is hired to carry out one component of a complex plan. Park Chang-yi is a dark-hearted, ruthless gangster that likes to carve people up with knives in a deadly ballet, his asymmetrical hairdo and long coat swirling through the air as the blood flies.

Opposing forces hear rumors of the plan that involves some sort of top secret map to a hidden treasure and decide to hire the services of Park "The Good" Do-won (Jung Woo-sung), a stolid cowboy who stops at nothing to hunt the bad guys down. His skills on a horse and with a Winchester are unrivaled.

Into the mix comes wild man Yoon "The Weird" Tae-goo (Song Kang-ho), a petty thief looking for a big score. He wants to stop living hand to mouth and be able to prop his boots up for a long nap in luxury.

When Yoon Tae-goo decides to rob a train, he unleashes not one, not two, but multiple groups of bad guys down on his own head. Humorously, he isn't always able to identify his enemies until it's almost too late.

Thus begins a crazy, action-packed, rollicking wild ride of a movie that will have you jumping out of your dusty leather La-Z-Boy and reaching for your six guns. Jaw-dropping gun battles, wide vista chases involving cars, trucks, horses, pipe smoking Mongolians, eye-popping stunts and visual effects make this a stupendous, must-see *Twistern.*

And you ain't seen anything yet, Cowpokes. The fun has just begun!

Unfortunately, all of this awesomeness didn't translate to a lick of profit in North America, grossing under $130,000, all due to poor marketing. Make that zero marketing. Fortunately, it carried some life in DVDs and via online streaming. The word of mouth was stupendous, with fans of raucous action passing the word like wildfire.

The rest of the world knew a good thing when it saw it, and, as of this writing, it has grossed well over $44 million worldwide, making it the second highest grossing Korean film of all time.

The cinematography, production, soundtrack and overall quality of this film are top notch. This movie is just gorgeous and a real credit to the *Twistern* subgenre. The $10 million budget may seem like pocket change in comparison to similar American movies, but it made *The Good, The Bad, The Weird* one of the most expensive Korean movies of all time. Not a dime seems to have been wasted, and there are surely budget control lessons to be learned here.

Pass me the kimchee and grilled rattler, Partner. Let's watch this *Twistern* again!

THE LEGEND OF GOD'S GUN

(2007)

Directed by Mike Bruce

Written by Mike Bruce and Kirkpatrick Thomas

Actors:

MIKE BRUCE
KIRKPATRICK THOMAS
DAVE KOENIG
JULIE PATTERSON
ROBERT BONES
SCOTT DYESWELL
SALLY FAY DALTON

Written, produced, filmed and acted by a bunch of Spaghetti Western-loving musicians, this movie has every detail of that subgenre, lovingly recreated. From the jump cuts, cinematography, costumes, and music (with a modern edge), it's a faithful homage.

A tale of revenge, the depressed sheriff of a small town must defend himself against a gang of dirty outlaws. Little do the outlaws know, but a gun-slinging preacher whose wife they murdered is on their trail. And finally, there's a doofus bounty hunter who has been hired to bring back the outlaws, dead or alive.

The whole thing's a bit of a mess. But, then, so were a lot of those old Spaghetti Westerns. Regardless, you have to give the dudes and dudettes of this production credit for the originality and effort of this psychedelic Western, produced with just a $30,000 budget and starring nobody you've ever heard of.

The plot is secondary here, but as is often the case, the visuals make up for whatever the acting and script lack. The humor is also along the lines of an inside joke. Most likely it was hilarious at the time, but as the viewer, we're left out. That's okay, because there's enough going on that the entertainment level is high.

A labor of love by the cast and crew, it's like watching a student film or a movie made by a bunch of kids with dad's camera (plus access to some seriously good video editing software). There's nothing professional about it, but it's still fun as all get out.

Most of the cast are musicians from the band Spindrift and there is a sudden, spontaneous music video of theirs mid-movie during an intermission, a sing- and stroll-along pop-rock song with a western twang. A music video by the group Gram Rabbit plays over the end credits, a creepy version of the psychedelic country rock song, "Devil's Playground".

From the movie poster: "You are about to leave this earth with many regrets." You won't have regrets when you see this *Twistern* on a lazy Sunday afternoon with your boots propped up and a cold sarsaparilla in your hand!

THE LIVING COFFIN

(1959)

Directed by Fernando Mendez
Screenplay by Ramon Obon

Actors:
GASTON SANTOS
MARIA DUVAL
PEDRO DE AGUILLION
CAROLINA BARRET
ANTONIO RAXEL
HORTENSIA SANTOVENA

An excellent example of the Mexican-made movies that blend the horror and Western genres, *The Living Coffin* (also known as *Scream of Death* and *El grito de la muerte*) is pure campy fun.

A lawman cowboy named Gaston (Gaston Santos), his sidekick, Coyote Loco (Pedro de Aguillon), and his hyper intelligent horse, Rayito, track the source of a mysterious statue to a cursed hacienda. Stolen corpses, murders, and a ghost called The Crying Woman have turned the once prosperous ranch into a financial ruin.

The Crying Woman is the spirit of a woman named Dona Clotilde (Carolina Barret), a widow who suffered the deaths of her two children before she went mad and died from anguish. She left behind her sister, Dona Maria, (Hortensia Santovena) and her niece, Maria Elana Garcia (Maria Duval).

When Dona Maria faints, a ranch hand is sent to retrieve the doctor (Antonio Raxel) from the deserted nearby town. As he takes a shortcut through a swamp, he's shot in the back.

Fortunately, Gaston and Coyote Loco are nearby and they carry him to his destination. They find that the doctor is liquored up at a bar and attempt to persuade him to return to his clinic.

When two strangers at the bar won't allow Gaston to remove the doctor, a brawl breaks out. The fight is amazingly acrobatic, flipping and slamming each other against a bar, a table, chairs, and the floor. In the end, our hero wins the day and he and the doctor hightail it out of there.

After the doctor patches the ranch hand up, they head back to the hacienda. But, mere seconds before they reach Dona Maria, she's brutally murdered by the gruesome walking corpse that was once her sister. They bury Dona Maria in a coffin with foot-thick stone walls, installing an electric alarm system, chaining and sealing the gates to the crypt.

After the death of Dona Maria, the doctor is despondent and starts to consume cognac at a steady pace in the study. After his second drink, he becomes the second victim of The Crying Woman and ends up hanging upside down in the fireplace, blood dripping down his face.

Will Gaston get to the bottom of what's going on? Will the lovely Maria Elana Garcia become the next victim? Will Coyote Loco ever get his desired nap? Is there a smarter, more capable horse than Rayito?

Mixing slapstick comedy, action and horror, director Fernando Mendez creates a wonderful, campy movie that features surprising twists and turns. While certainly not his most accomplished or even famous work, *The Living Coffin* mixes the style of Edgar Allen Poe with Scooby Doo shenanigans.

The visually intriguing cast mixed with the low budget makeup and effects really make this a classic *Twistern* to take a gander at. Just don't ignore that crypt alarm if it rings!

THE PROPOSITION

(2005)

Directed by John Hillcoat
Written by Nick Cave

Actors:
GUY PEARCE
RAY WINSTONE
DANNY HUSTON
EMILY WATSON
JOHN HURT
DAVID GULPILIL
RICHARD WILSON
DAVID WENHAM
TOMMY LEWIS II

Charlie Burns (Guy Pearce) and his younger brother, Mikey (Richard Wilson) are the only survivors when police attack his gang of hooligans. Captain Stanley (Ray Winstone) offers Charlie a trade – seek out and kill his older brother Arthur (Danny Huston) in exchange for a stay of execution for Mikey and a full pardon.

Charlie sets out on the long ride to track down Arthur, who is hiding out in the bleak Australian mountains with several compatriots. When he stops to rest at a desert bar, he discovers that the inhabitants have all been slain by local aboriginals, except for one old grizzled fellow by the name of Jellon Lamb (John Hurt). Lamb is prone to spout drunken, flowery prose and it soon becomes clear to Charlie that he is a bounty hunter also in pursuit of Arthur. So he knocks him out and leaves him unconscious at the bar.

As Charlie draws closer to Arthur's hideaway, he's attacked by an aboriginal tribe and takes a spear to the chest. As he loses consciousness, he sees that someone has come to his rescue and has counter-attacked the tribe.

Meanwhile, Captain Stanley continues his quest to clean up the rough Australian outback. The reason for all his hard work is revealed when we are introduced to his fragile wife, Martha (Emily Watson). The Burns gang is accused of brutally murdering the Hopkins family, including a pregnant woman. The vicious slaying haunts both the Captain and his wife Martha, in particular. She has nightmares of the dead unborn child and her need for comfort from her husband is unrequited as he throws himself into the job of hunting the perpetrator, Arthur Burns.

Captain Stanley is ordered by his peacock of a boss, Eden Fletcher (David Wenham) to flog Mikey. Stanley sees this as a short-term solution to appease the townsfolk that risks killing Mikey, and worse, unraveling his plan to force Charlie to bring Arthur to justice.

Will Charlie succeed in killing his psychotic older brother? Will Captain Stanley be functionally hogtied by his boss? Will Martha break like a porcelain doll?

Stunningly filmed on location, director John Hillcoat paints a gritty, brutal, and accurate picture of the outback in the 1880s, a place where high society is like a fresh water fountain in the middle of the desert. Punctuated by alternative music singer/songwriter Nick Cave's haunting soundtrack (who also wrote the screenplay), Arthur Burns is a mythical, horrific, nightmarish beast. Is he the spawn of Satan? How do you stop someone who is practically a ghost?

The Proposition is an independent film with a budget of $20 million, but it never received much publicity outside of its native country. As a result, it didn't make a profit. Possibly the finest *Twistern* ever made, don't let this doggie slip the lasso. Do yourself a favor and see it!

The tagline read, "This land will be civilized." But not without a lot of bloodshed, cowboy!

THE STRANGERS GUNDOWN

(1969)

Directed by Sergio Garrone
Written by Sergio Garrone and Anthony Steffen

Actors:
ANTHONY STEFFEN
PAOLO GOZLINO
LUCIANO ROSSI
RADO RASSIMOV
TEODORO CORRA
JEAN LOUIS
CARLO GADDI
THOMAS RUDI
LUCIA BOMEZ
EMY ROSSI SCOTTI

Also known as *Django the Bastard,* this seemingly standard Spaghetti Western is more than what it appears. In fact, it has all of the hallmarks of a really decent, slow-paced horror movie where the killer is more than human and slays his increasingly panicked victims at his leisure.

A mysterious cowboy clothed in all black strolls unnoticed into the center of town and drives a funereal cross into the ground. On it is the name of a man and the date of his death. Trouble is, the man is still alive and the date is today…

The story of a betrayed soldier (Anthony Steffen, who also co-wrote) who was murdered by his back-stabbing superiors, this shoot 'em up is a tale of revenge; while the bad guys live in luxury, we're led to believe that he's literally been to Hell and back. Is he still human or is he some demon sent from the depths of Hades?

His main target is the officer that killed him, Rod Murdok (Paolo Gozlino). Now a wealthy rancher, Rod doesn't really care about any human life other than his own. By Rod's side is his brother Jack (Luciano Rossi), a deranged psychopath who takes great joy in others' pain and suffering. Also present is Jack's wife Alida (Rada Rassimov), a money-hungry narcissist who ends up aiding the mysterious stranger for her own devious motives.

The cinematography is superb, with men frantically trying to find Django while he stands right in their midst, ghostlike. The plot creeps steadily along, building tension in the best horror movie tradition. Rossi's character is particularly disturbing and he does a great job plumbing the depths of his psychosis in his brief moments onscreen. The bad guys are truly slimy, and there's a great scene where two of them play a fun game of catch while everyone watches and place bets on who will be the last to be caught holding a lit stick of dynamite! These are the folks your mother warned you about.

Django is a character name that recurs throughout Western movie history. There are quite a few films that use it and several of these films are worth seeking out, Mario Lanfranchi's *Django* being an example of a good one. The name wasn't always exclusive to Italian Westerns, either. It also captured the imagination of a few German filmmakers.

Unlike the "standard" Spaghetti Westerns, *The Strangers Gundown* could have just as easily been made by a horror maestro. Just pray you don't stroll down the center of town and come across your own headstone…

"From Hell…the Stranger comes back!"

THE TERROR OF TINY TOWN

(1938)

Directed by Sam Newfield

Written by Fred Myton

Actors:
BILLY CURTIS
YVONNE MORAY
BAT HAINES
BILLY PLATT
JOHN T BAMBURY
JOSEPH HERBST
CHARLES BECKER
NITA KREBS

You know you're in for a treat when a man stands in front of a velvet curtain and announces that you're about to see a "novelty picture."

Buck Lawson (Billy Curtis) is the son of a local cattle rancher and the good guy. You can tell because he wears all white and rides a white horse. Billy Rhodes (Bat Haines) is his nefarious nemesis, who tries to pit the Lawson clan against their neighbors, the Prestons, to gain control of the area. We're pretty sure he's the bad guy because he's wearing all black and rides a black Shetland.

What? The man rides a…Shetland? You mean those tiny horses that you see in parades? Yep, Tex, that's correct.

Did I forget to mention that this movie is entirely populated by little people (including several that appeared as Munchkins in *The Wizard of Oz*)? Oh, and that it's a musical?

Gadzooks!

Now, the musical element is not new. The fabulous Gene Autry laid down the groundwork for the classic singing cowboy. The combination of the singing and the all little person cast is certainly novel, but here it's played for lighthearted humor. The set was intentionally left "normal" sized and there are classic scenes of various characters entering the saloon not through the swinging doors, but under them.

Billy rides around causing havoc, while Nancy Preston (Yvonne Moray) and Buck Lawson are out prancing around together on the prairie. A Romeo and Juliet-type plot thread is revealed, culminating in the inevitable hand-to-hand fight for Nancy's hand between Billy and Buck that literally ends with a bang.

The plot is standard fare and the uniqueness of the film relies on the visual qualities of the cast and the musical numbers.

Several of the actors are actually not bad and it would have been interesting to watch their careers if they had been given the opportunity to work with roles that actually let them develop their characters and their craft. Little folks are not often given acting opportunities, and *The Terror of Tiny Town* most likely wasn't the best of platforms to further their careers.

Billy Curtis has real charisma that's palatable in the first half of the film. But, it dwindles in the second half, for some reason. He may not have been all that comfortable with the singing. But he's darn good at posing with a twinkle in his eye and a tip of the ten gallon (or is it pint?) hat to the ladies.

You can catch a couple of the actors again as Munchkins in *The Wizard of Oz,* which was released the following year. Sam

Newfield went on to be one of the most prolific American directors ever, with nearly 300 films over a 30-year-plus career.

Announcer: "Ladies and gentlemen and children of all ages, we're going to present for your approval a novelty picture with an all midget cast, the first of it's kind to ever be produced. I'm told that it has everything, that is, everything that a Western should have."

It does, so saddle up, tiny cowpokes!

THE VALLEY OF GWANGI

(1969)

Directed by Jim O'Connolly
Screenplay by William Bast

Actors:
JAMES FRANCISCUS
GILA GOLAN
RICHARD CARLSON
CURTIS ARDEN
LAURENCE NAISMITH
FREDA JACKSON
GUSTAVO ROJO

Tuck Kirby (James Franciscus) is a real hustler, always looking to make a buck. In the past, he was part of a traveling Wild West Show, but he got involved with the star attraction, spitfire TJ Breckenridge (Gila Golan) and left her in the lurch (possibly at the altar). TJ's special act is that she jumps her horse Owen off a high platform into a little pool.

Buffalo Bill has contracted Tuck to buy Owen from TJ, but she's headstrong and having none of it. Besides, she has an ace up her sleeve – a tiny horse no bigger than a cat! What she doesn't know is the tiny horse is actually a prehistoric Eohippus, the earliest known horse that existed 50 million years ago, supposedly long extinct.

Tuck befriends a paleontologist named Horace Bromley (Laurence Naismith) who sees the Eohippus and tells Tuck what it is. But Tuck is not about to turn his back on TJ again, so he vows to tell her exactly what she has. Before he can, the Eohippus is stolen by the group of gypsies who originally took it from "The Forbidden

Valley." Tuck sees them and gives chase, along with the paleontologist, TJ, and her posse.

They chase the gypsies back to the valley and guess what they discover? Dinosaurs! Forgotten by time for the past 50 million years, they run across a selection of scary critters, all of whom seem intent on eating each other– but haven't yet.

Does it make sense? No! Does it make for a fun movie? You betcha!

There are some additional preposterously delightful elements included here, including but not limited to, a token Gypsy little person for no reason, a blind witch that gets around just fine for a sightless person (how does she keep her eye patch on without any strings?), the creepy paleontologist that has an unnatural liking for young boys, an elephant (at a Wild West Show?), and the fact that we never see more than one of each kind of dinosaur. How did they procreate?

The amazing Ray Harryhausen provides the stop motion animation and this is his last prehistoric-themed film. In the age of CGI, this time intensive way of creating special effects is almost a lost art. Although dated, it's a lot of fun to watch and appreciate the monsters as they stutter step through their scenes.

Shot on location in Spain, the desert scenery is gorgeous and you can almost feel the dust on your skin. The soundtrack by Jerome Moross is dynamic and classic. There are several horse stunts that are painful to watch, with the animal actually rolling over the rider. It's amazing that nobody died.

Originally planned as a follow-up to the 1933 *King Kong*, there are several plot similarities here, including the final showdown. Instead of a tall building with a gigantic monkey dangling from it, we get a Mexican church with a T-Rex smashing its mammoth tail into gothic pillars. It's all great fun.

Imagine the first pitch meeting for this movie, "Hey, what we need is a cowboy and dinosaur movie!" Unfortunately, that was during the decline of the creature feature and this movie never got the attention that it deserved.

Still, this has got to be the King of all cowboy and dinosaur films (quick, name a dozen!) and a must see.

The movie poster declared, "Cowboys battle monsters in the lost world of Forbidden Valley!" They sure do!

THE VILLIAN

(1979)

Directed by Hal Needham
Written by Robert G. Kane

Actors:
KIRK DOUGLAS
ARNOLD SCHWARZENEGGER
ANN-MARGRET
PAUL LYNDE
STROTHER MARTIN
ROBERT TESSIER
MEL TILLIS

Do you lie awake at night dreaming of impossibly whacky movie themes? Me too! Isn't insomnia horrible?

Here's a doozy of a kooky premise. What if we had a huge star, somebody like Kirk Douglas, play Wily E. Coyote in the live action version of the Warner Brothers *Roadrunner* cartoon? Yeah!

And what if we cast a brand new actor with an impossibly thick and out of place accent in the role of Roadrunner? How about the famous bodybuilder, Arnold Schwarzenegger? Perfect! And we could dress him in baby blue, polyester Western duds. You betcha, cowboy!

Unfortunately, none of that could happen. We might get Schwarzenegger. He's obviously interested in building his acting resume. But, Douglas? Never!

Ah…anything is possible in the loco world of *Twisterns.* Dreams do come true (or is that nightmares?) and all of the above ended up gracing the silver screen. Director Hal Needham brought this outlandish concept together, and it actually has real moments of hilarity.

Aspiring bad guy, Cactus Jack Slade (Kirk Douglas), opens the shenanigans by attempting to rob a moving train using the ingenious method of jumping off a cliff onto the roof. Of course, he misses and ends up flat on his face on the tracks, the dust of the passing locomotive settling around him. Just like the original cartoon, with a complete disregard to physics, he gets up, dusts himself off, and rides his horse to the next town to rob a bank.

While Cactus Jack attempts to blow the safe, flirtatious Charming Jones (Ann-Margret) arrives in town, chaperoned by the polyester clad, handsome stranger named…Handsome Stranger (Arnold Schwarzenegger) to run an errand of importance for her father. Unfortunately, her scoundrel of an uncle doesn't want her to succeed in her task, so he hires Cactus Jack to stop her. Of course, Cactus Jack devises all sorts of elaborate and ever more ridiculous ways to do so, all of which are inadvertently foiled by Handsome Stranger.

In the beginning, the movie enjoyably deviates from the original cartoon that it's based on. But, somewhere along the way the confrontations become more brief and ludicrous, to the point that the entire works just sort of fizzles out, ending in an a finale that is not worthy of the first half of the movie.

Still, that first half is highly enjoyable and well worth the weak ending. This is meant to be light-hearted fun, and it is. The actors are clearly enjoying their silly roles, including Paul Lynde (in his last movie role) as Nervous Elk, the Indian chief who sees opportunity in the moronic maneuvers of Cactus Jack.

Unsurprisingly, the movie was a flop in the States. When it was released overseas, the title was changed to *Cactus Jack*. I'm sure that made a huge difference and audiences flocked to it…or, not. Neither Douglas nor Schwarzenegger have made another theatrically released Western to date. This endeavor might have been just enough for them. Or, maybe they just fired their agents and found new ones that kept them out of turkeys like this one.

Still, if you want an outlandishly whacky, light comedy *Twistern,* you could certainly do worse! Make this a double feature with the TV movie *Evil Roy Slade,* starring John Astin. There is no connection between the two productions or characters, but the similarities are numerous. This is fun for preteen and adult cowpokes with a slapstick sense of humor.

The movie poster proclaimed, "...the fastest fun in the West!" Th-th- th- that's all, folks!

THE WARRIOR'S WAY

(2010)

Directed by Sngmoo Lee
Written by Sngmoo Lee

Actors:
DONG-GUN JANG
KATE BOSWORTH
DANNY HUSTON
GEOFFREY RUSH
TONY COX
LUNG TI

"Okay, you settled down? You got your ears open? This is the story of the sad flute, a laughing baby, a weeping sword. A long long time ago, in a land far far away, there lived a warrior. A warrior with empty eyes," says the town drunk, Ronald (Geoffrey Rush).

After wiping out an entire enemy clan, a Chinese assassin encounters the final, surviving member – an infant princess. Instead of finishing the job of total annihilation, he decides to protect her at all costs. The greatest danger now comes from the people who raised and trained him.

He narrowly escapes with the baby and journeys to America, where a friend has settled in the Old West. When he arrives, he finds that his friend is no longer among the living. The tumble weed town where his friend lived is inhabited by a circus and is under siege by a band of murderous cowboys. Still, it seems like a good place to hide out, away from the far-reaching clutches of his pursuers.

He assumes the identity and job of his deceased pal, who ran a laundry. The circus folk grow to like him, particularly a young woman named Lynne (Kate Bosworth). He likes her too, but he's also a cold-blooded killer, which doesn't make him exactly warm and cuddly. Lynne keeps at it, though, and she sees the good in him, somewhere deep inside his soul.

Soon, she learns of his past and he of hers. Her family was brutally slain by the evil cowboy gang and she was nearly raped by the leader, The Colonel (Danny Huston). Fortunately, she injured him gravely, enough to get rid of him temporarily.

Bad guys like The Colonel always come back. That's a *Twistern* law. They're just ornery cusses and they always have an axe to grind. Instead of pursuing a pleasant hobby like underwater basket weaving or scrapbooking, they're bound and determined to make life miserable for everyone around them.

The Colonel and his gang reappear and the big showdown is on. But wouldn't you know it, when they force the assassin to defend himself and the circus folk, it alerts his old clan, who come to kill him and the baby princess.

The Warrior's Way is a great mix of action, spectacular visuals, Western cues, Asian martial arts, and the absurdity of a circus side show in an abandoned Old West ghost town. Like *Jonah Hex,* this is escapist stuff and a wild *Twistern.* Predictably, it was also a box office disaster in 2010, just like *Hex.* Made for $42 million, it grossed $11 million. That's too bad, because it really is an entertaining movie, especially for fans that enjoy all of the elements mentioned.

This was director Sngmoo Lee's first effort and, hopefully, not his last. His control of the production is epic and there are many, many interesting touches. For example, all of the bad guys (and there are a lot of bad guys) are literally faceless, adding a real air of strangeness to the already odd scenario. No detail is left untouched; everything is given its own unique quality. *The Warrior's Way* will live on as a *Twistern* cult classic.

Ronald wisely says, "The warrior learned there's a heck of a lot more pleasure making things grow, than there is in cutting them down."

Don't miss this sword-swingin' *Twistern*!

THE WHITE BUFFALO

(1977)

Directed by J. Lee Thompson
Written by Richard Sale

Actors:
CHARLES BRONSON
JACK WARDEN
WILL SAMPSON
KIM NOVAC
SLIM PICKENS
JOHN CARRADINE
ED LAUTER
RICHARD GILLILAND
CLINT WALKER

You know you're in for something special when you see the name of executive producer Dino De Laurentiis combined with the sounds of a perfectly ominous soundtrack by famed composer John Barry.

Surrealistic mountainous scenes form a backdrop for a giant, demonic white buffalo, who roars and charges from the depths of Hades. This is the nightmare that haunts Wild Bill Hickok (Charles Bronson), who is traveling by train under the assumed name of James Otis to escape his checkered past and hunt down the mystical creature from his tortured dreams.

When he arrives at his destination, a frontier town, he's met by a range of characters including the blood-thirsty military officer Tom Custer (Ed Lauter). A bar fight erupts. Hickock escapes by a stagecoach driven by Abel Pickney (Slim Pickens). A shyster and his equally questionable female companion are fellow passengers. Along the way, they discover two dead men and are shot at by a

Native American. In the gun battle, Hickok's traveling companions are killed, but he and Pickney escape.

At the end of their journey lies another frontier town, where Hickok and his old flame, "Poker" Jenny Schermerhorn (Kim Novac) reunite after many years. But he has no time for her. He's a man haunted by the vision of the white buffalo and is driven to destroy it before it destroys him.

Meanwhile, a Native American village is ravaged by the white buffalo of Hickok's fantastical slumbering phantasms. Their leader, Crazy Horse (Will Sampson), takes the death of a young girl personally and seeks revenge on the marauding bison. This confirms that the creature is in fact real, not just Hickok's hallucination.

Will Hickock and Crazy Horse battle to the death? Or will they meet their demise at the horns of the white buffalo?

The White Buffalo is often compared to the classic film that made us all afraid to dip our toes in the kiddie pool at Aunt Selma's...*Jaws.* And in some ways, it is similar in that it is a creature feature and the filmmakers do a good job not showing the scary monster too much, allowing our imaginations to fill in the gaps and shadows. Unfortunately, a shark is a fearsome critter and a buffalo isn't. I suppose if you're a field of grass and you don't want to be eaten or if you're stupid enough to step into the path of a stampede, there might be some looseness in your bladder. But here, despite some ominous sound effects and a truly hairy visage, the buffalo is just not that scary. He's too big, too slow (in reality), and too noisy. A shark can just sneak right up on you and nip your nellys right off as you practice your doggy paddle.

So, that's not really the draw in this psychedelic *Twistern* with horror genre overtones. No, it's the cast, plain and simple. And they *are* fun to gander at! Scrape up a couple of pesos and go on an adventure with Charles Bronson in *The White Buffalo*!

"Charging...roaring...breathing fire and Hell. The white earthquake is here!" promised the movie poster. Saddle up for a monster *Twistern*!

TIMERIDER:
THE ADVENTURES OF LYLE SWANN

(1982)

Directed by William Dear
Written by Michael Nesmith

Actors:
FRED WARD
PETER COYOTE
BELINDA BAUER
ED LAUTER
RICHARD MASUR
TRACEY WALTER
L.Q. JONES
CHRIS MULKEY

Off in the distance, the sound of a dirt bike buzzes like an angry hornet. The rider, Lyle Swann (Fred Ward), reads the desert like a book, jumping off low hills, sliding in the dirt, and navigating rocks like they were nothing. Using his high-tech helmet, he's able to listen to music, communicate with his crew and instantly analyze the terrain ahead.

Simultaneously, a group of scientists are running an top secret experiment. A monkey is sent into the future using a device presumably isolated in the same part of the desert that Lyle races his motorcycle in.

When tumbleweeds repeatedly trigger an alert at the lab, the scientists ignore the warning. When Lyle happens to ride right next to the time travel machine, it transports him to the year 1877, unbeknownst to the scientists. When he arrives, he runs afoul of Porter Reese (Peter Coyote) and his evil gang of cutthroats, featuring the brothers Dorsett: Claude (Richard Masur) and Carl (Tracey Walter). They've seen Lyle's bike and though they fear it, they see it as a weapon and want it for themselves.

Lyle holes up in San Marcos, where he meets the padre (Ed Lauter) and an alluring woman named Claire Cygne (Belinda Bauer). Reese and his gang follow Lyle to the town and when two Marshalls (veteran actors L.Q. Jones and Chris Mulkey) show up to apprehend Reese, a gunfight erupts. In the hail of lead, Carl gets his nose blown off by Claire. In retaliation, Reese and his gang kidnap her and steal Lyle's motorcycle. A posse is formed and they go hell for leather after them.

Viewers will be delighted by the clichéd 80s production. And yet, *Timerider: The Adventures of Lyle Swann* rises above. All credit is given to the tremendous cast for working with a rather simplistic and trite script. Somehow, they make the predictable enjoyable and bring one-dimensional characters to life with aplomb.

Another interesting aspect of the film is Michael Nesmith's (of *Monkees* fame) ahead-of-its-time soundtrack that mixes hard rock and country music with action movie cues. Strangely, the soundtrack for *Timerider* was not available until 18 years after the film's release. Nesmith also wrote and produced the film.

The DVD release has a few small changes in editing. While not a game changer, try to see the theatrical release, which was eventually also released in DVD format. Fans know that it contains the famous "boot scene," a tiny bit of gore that adds a wonderfully cheesy special effect to the finale.

So, crank up the time machine in your barn and prepare for a fun *Twistern,* 1980s style!

"You shot it. What a bunch of dumb sons of bitches, you shot it! A machine, you butt-heads!" screams Porter Reese.

UNDEAD OR ALIVE

(2007)

Directed by Glasgow Phillips

Written by Glasgow Phillips and Scott Pourroy

Actors:
CHRIS KATTAN
JAMES DENTON
MATT BESSER
NAVI RAWAT
CHRIS COPPOLA
LESLIE JORDAN

"Guns don't kill people. Zombies kill people."

Rustle up this little doggie...*Undead or Alive: A Zombedy*!

Chris Kattan (*Saturday Night Live*) and James Denton (*Desperate Housewives*) star in this highly enjoyable lighthearted direct-to-DVD Western horror comedy.

An Army deserter named Elmer (Denton) and a lovelorn washout cowboy named Luke (Kattan) steal a load of cash from an evil sheriff. The ensuing high-jinks take a turn for the better as it becomes clear that, due to a Native American curse, there's a zombie apocalypse afoot. Making off with the loot is the least of Elmer and Luke's problems when they need to avoid being eaten.

This is a fun movie, if you're in the mood for silly high jinks, and there's plenty of funny dialogue and entertaining action sequences. They obviously had a lot of fun making it, and if you can get in the swing of the shenanigans, then you'll have a good time. There is some gore, but it's not terrifically grotesque. The film pokes gentle fun at the zombie genre as well as Westerns, making it a worthy *Twistern.*

Matt Besser (*Upright Citizen's Brigade*) as Sheriff Claypool nearly steals the show. His over-the-top performance really gets this shindig hopping. The role of Geronimo's (the originator of the zombie curse) niece is played by Navi Rawat (*Numb3rs*), who will be one to watch in future projects. Her character is a bit underdeveloped but she does a lot with what she has to work with.

Director Glasgow Phillips does a good job with the minimal budget. His credits include writing for the infamous animated TV show *South Park,* which gives you a fairly good idea of where the humor is coming from in *Undead or Alive.* The budget was relatively low here, yet nothing indicates a hurried or slapdash production (with the possible exclusion of some rather cheesy explosion special effects). The gore, the zombie makeup and the sets are well done.

Undead or Alive was clearly made by a group of folks that truly enjoyed what they were doing and it deserves a cult following. Add this one to your *Twistern* movie queue!

WESTWORLD

(1973)

Directed by Michael Crichton
Written by Michael Crichton

Actors:
YUL BRYNNER
RICHARD BENJAMIN
JAMES BROLIN
DICK VAN PATTEN

John Blane (James Brolin) convinces his buddy Peter Martin (Richard Benjamin) to go with him to a high-tech vacation planet called Delos. Vacationers are given the choice of three theme parks: sword-swinging MedievalWorld, toga-wearing RomanWorld, or gun-slinging WesternWorld. They choose the last option.

Peter is highly skeptical, but John assures him that this is a vacation like no other, where he will experience the reality of the Old West. They'll get to brawl in a bar, go to a bordello, and have a shootout at high noon.

They arrive and are given full costumes, including guns. WesternWorld is populated with realistic robots that are programmed to interact with the guests, providing anything they want, from sexual encounters to being murdered.

One of the robots in WesternWorld is designed to challenge guests to a duel, which he will always lose. But something goes horribly wrong and the robot ends up still standing after his duel with John, killing him. Peter is in shock and runs from the malfunctioning robot, which proceeds to attempt to hunt him down.

The dueling robot, called The Gunslinger, is played by Yul Brynner and references his iconic role from *The Magnificent Seven*. His stone cold face as he mercilessly tracks Peter down surely helped inspire Arnold Schwarzenegger's character in *Terminator.* Famed horror movie director John Carpenter supposedly based his serial killer Michael Myers in *Halloween* on Brynner's portrayal of The Gunslinger.

This was also the first movie that used digital images in a big budget production. The Gunslinger's viewpoint was created by painstakingly color separating each frame, then scanning them to convert them into rectangular blocks and adjusting the color values to create a blocky, pixilated image. This was pretty cutting-edge for the day, and the effect is impressive.

This was Michael Crichton's first feature film as director and writer. He would go on to direct and write several other interesting sci-fi films including *Coma* and *Runaway.* But his real success came from writing some of the biggest bestselling fiction novels of all time, most of which have been turned into blockbusters such as *Jurassic Park, Rising Sun, Sphere,* and *The 13th Warrior.*

Composer Fred Karlin creates an aurally fascinating mix of Western movie score and electronic music.

Westworld was such a box office success, that it inspired a successor, *Futureworld.* An all-new cast was brought in, with the exception of Yul Brynner who returns in his original role. While the sequel is not quite as good as the original, it featured another interesting group of actors, including Peter Fonda, Blythe Danner, and Arthur Hill. There was also a short-lived TV series, called *Beyond Westworld.*

There are a lot of classic Western themes explored in *Westworld,* as well as some classic science fiction elements, including the exploration of author Isaac Asimov's Three Laws of Robotics, which are:

1. A robot may not injure a human being or, through inaction, allow a human being to come to harm.
2. A robot must obey the orders given to it by human beings, except where such orders would conflict with the First Law.
3. A robot must protect its own existence as long as such protection does not conflict with the First or Second Laws.

Abide by the laws and take a gander at this classic, must-see *Twistern*.

WILD WILD WEST

(1999)

Directed by Barry Sonnenfeld

Story by Jim Thomas and John Thomas

Actors:

WILL SMITH
KEVIN KLINE
KENNETH BRANAGH
SALMA HAYEK
TED LEVINE
M EMMET WALSH
MUSETTA VANDER
BAI LING
GARY CARLOS CERVANTES

When ex-Confederate General "Bloodbath" McGrath (Ted Levine) starts kidnapping the top scientists of the day with the intent of building a super weapon to overthrow the government, Army Captain James "Jim" West (Will Smith) and U.S. Marshall Artemus "Artie" Gordon (Kevin Kline) are sent to stop him.

West and Gordon set off for New Orleans in the President of the United States' train, *The Wanderer*, a private train fitted with ejector chairs, hidden compartments, a laboratory, and other seemingly incongruous amenities.

They track McGrath to a large, extravagant party where the real enemy is a legless evil genius named Dr. Arliss Loveless (Kenneth Branagh). In an act of brutality, Loveless murders McGrath and all of his men in a demonstration of his newest weapon, a steam-powered tank.

A sultry singer by the name of Rita Escobar (Salma Hayek) joins them in their quest to rescue the scientists. One of the hostages is her beloved father, Dr. Guillermo Escobar (Gary Carlos Cervantes).

Set in the year 1869, *Wild Wild West* incorporates several "steampunk" elements, a genre that elements of science fiction and Victorian-era fashion. The fun visual gags and weapons go far beyond the standard Western fare.

After the success of *Men in Black,* director Barry Sonnenfeld brought the same, big-budget slickness and raucous humor that worked so well before. Unfortunately, it doesn't work as well here, mainly due to the urban qualities of Will Smith's performance. Smith stated that he was not happy with the film. It's not that he isn't a huge personality and a charismatic actor. He is. It just seems that while all of the other actors are playing characters, he seems to be, well, playing Will Smith. His comic timing is as enjoyable as ever, but it's out of place in this setting.

Don't miss Musetta Vander's (of the *Oblivion* movies) small role.

One of the creators of the original television series *The Wild Wild West,* Gilbert Ralston, sued Warner Brothers over a rights dispute involving intellectual property. Unfortunately, he passed away before the suit could be settled. Warner Brothers ended up settling with his family for a large amount of money.

There have been rumors of reviving the television series. Let's hope that project gets made and that it pays proper homage to the original that starred Robert Conrad and Ross Martin. Fans of the original should consider this movie treatment an entity unto itself.

The television show and the movie are not comparable; even if we desperately want to see the characters again.

Though the film received generally negative reviews, *Wild Wild West* is a *Twistern* full of fun action sequences and genuinely funny dialogue. This isn't a film for a MENSA party, but it's a good time.

As President Grant said to James West, "...not every situation calls for your patented approach of 'shoot first, shoot later, shoot some more and then when everybody's dead try to ask a question or two.'"

Take a shot at this fun *Twistern* action comedy!

ZACHARIAH

(1971)

Directed by George Englund

Written by Philip Austin, Peter Bergman, Joe Massot, David Ossman and Phil Proctor

Actors:
JOHN RUBINSTEIN
DON JOHNSON
COUNTRY JOE MCDONALD
DOUG KERSHAW
ELVIN JONES
WILLIAM CHALLEE
DICK VAN PATTEN
PATRICIA QUINN

Billed as the first "electric" Western, *Zachariah* is the story of a young man (John Rubenstein) who mail-orders a pistol. When it arrives, he teaches himself how to shoot and decides that he wants to be a gunfighter. When he informs his best friend, Matthew (Don Johnson), the two ride off to join a gang of stagecoach robbers named The Crackers (real life musicians Country Joe and the Fish) who also happen to be a hippy rock band. In the process, Zachariah successfully guns down a man in a duel.

After watching The Crackers botch robbery after robbery, Zachariah and Matthew devise a scheme where the band performs a concert from the back of a wagon as a distraction while they rob a bank. The plan works, encouraging Zachariah to desire more than just the hand-to-mouth existence that the musicians are clearly content with. At first, Matthew is reluctant to leave the life they have grown accustomed to, but in the end he sticks with his friend and they set out for adventures unknown.

Zachariah learns about a mysterious gunfighter who goes by the handle of Job Cain (Elvin Jones) and decides that is where they need to focus their attentions. When they track him down, the inevitable confrontation ends up in a battle not with the experienced killer, but between the two best friends. Zachariah is sure that there will be a point where he and Matthew will have to duel each other. He can't accept that and so he chooses to leave. Matthew is distraught, but sees a future with Job Cain and the two part ways.

Zachariah is heartbroken and rides west. Near the border, he stumbles across an old hermit (William Challee) who takes him in, teaching him pacifism. But Zachariah's wandering spirit pulls at his soul, so he saddles up and rides the rest of the way to Belle Starr's (Patricia Quinn) desert oasis brothel.

Zachariah woos Belle and they become romantically entwined. Zachariah is swept up in the whirlpool of emotions, but that wandering spirit still controls him and he leaves.

Having no better place to go, he returns to the old man's simple ranch. Feeling lost and forlorn, he accepts the offer to learn the secrets of the desert. In the dust and prairie brush, he discovers a love for life and rejects his violent past.

Will he return to his old ways? What will happen to Matthew in the presence of the serpentine Job Cain? Will the two friends reunite and mend their broken hearts?

Imagine *Jesus Christ Superstar* mixed with a classic Western and you've got *Zachariah,* a full-blown hippy experience straight out of the 1970s. There are so many incongruous elements in the movie, including characters using electric guitars and outrageous costumes that are groovier than gaucho.

Writer Joe Massot and members of the comedy troupe The Firesign Theater created *Zachariah* as a musical *Twistern* that parodies Herman Hesse's book *Siddhartha*. Much of the dialogue is nearly a direct quote.

Many of the cast are musicians: drummer Elvin Jones played with jazz pioneer John Coltrane, country fiddler Doug Kershaw has a cameo and the hermit's musical accompaniment is the psychedelic rock duo White Lightnin'. Interestingly, not every scene is a musical number and there is plenty of dialogue, story, and character development as a result. Sadly, the soundtrack is out of print.

Stunning scenery and far out psychedelic rock punctuate this tale of true friendship set in the Old West. Don't miss a baby-faced Don Johnson in his second feature film role and John Rubenstein as Zachariah; as the movie poster tagline read, he was "A Head of His Time."

Groovy, cowpokes! It's time for a psychedelic, rock musical *Twistern*, so strap on your bellbottoms, fluff your afro and flash the peace sign. Let's ride!

TWISTERNS ORGANIZED BY GENRE

ANIMATED
Rango

COMEDY
Back to the Future Part III
Blazing Saddles
Lust in the Dust
Oblivion
Oblivion 2: Backlash
Rango
Rustler's Rhapsody
Straight to Hell
Sundown: The Vampire in Retreat
The Apple Dumpling Gang
The Terror of Tiny Town
The Villain
Undead or Alive
Wild Wild West
Zachariah

FOREIGN
El Topo
Red Hill
Red Sun
Renegade
Sukiyaki Western Django
Tears of the Black Tiger
The Good The Bad The Weird
The Living Coffin
The Proposition

HORROR

Billy the Kid vs. Dracula
Curse of the Undead
Dead Birds
From Dusk Till Dawn 3: The Hangman's Daughter
Ghost Town
Grim Prairie Tales
Jessie James Meets Frankenstein's Daughter
Jonah Hex
Near Dark
Ravenous
Red Hill
Sundown: The Vampire in Retreat
The Burrowers
The Dead and the Damned
The Living Coffin
The Strangers Gundown
The Valley of Gwangi
The White Buffalo
Undead or Alive

MUSICALS

Lust in the Dust
Rustler's Rhapsody
Stingray Sam
Zachariah

PSYCHEDELIC
Dead Man
Dudes
El Topo
Jonah Hex
North Star
Renegade
Straight to Hell
The Legend of God's Gun
The Proposition
The White Buffalo
Zachariah

SCIENCE FICTION
Back to the Future Part III
Cowboys and Aliens
Oblivion
Oblivion 2: Backlash
Outland
Serenity
Stingray Sam
Timerider: The Adventures of Lyle Swann
Westworld

ABOUT THE AUTHOR

Trained as a filmmaker and graphic designer, Kelly Knight chose instead to follow his other lifelong passion, the martial arts. He teaches a variety of traditional and modern martial arts at his school outside of Philadelphia, Pennsylvania. He makes small, zero budget, independent movies and continues to write.

Mr. Knight would like to acknowledge the help and support of the following people, without whom this book would not have been possible: Helen Gelstine, Aaron Gelstine, Stu Dunn, and Margaret Caracappa.

This book is dedicated to his wife, Nancy, the purtiest cowgirl on the prairie.

Visit us online at Twistern.com for more *Twistern* culture.

"Let's ride!"

www.ingramcontent.com/pod-product-compliance
Lightning Source LLC
LaVergne TN
LVHW012332100826
845148LV00017B/2118

* 9 7 8 0 6 1 5 6 2 4 7 2 3 *